More Ser[illegible] Diff[illegible]ult Subjects

Background Information, Sermon Ideas, Stories and Thoughts to Take Away

Edited by John Cox

www.kevinmayhew.com

First published in Great Britain in 2013 by Kevin Mayhew Ltd
Buxhall, Stowmarket, Suffolk IP14 3BW
Tel: +44 (0) 1449 737978 Fax: +44 (0) 1449 737834
E-mail: info@kevinmayhewltd.com

www.kevinmayhew.com

ISBN 978 1 84867 587 2
Catalogue No. 1501389

Cover design by Rob Mortonson
© Image used under licence from Shutterstock Inc
Edited by John Cox; copy-edited by Linda Ottewell
Typeset by Richard Weaver

Printed and bound in Great Britain

Contents

Foreword

There were always more difficult subjects than could be covered in the first book, *Sermons on Difficult Subjects,* so a further 72 subjects are considered here, ranging from Abortion to Wealth, Fraud to Promiscuity. We said in the first Foreword that we would include Superstition in a second book, so you will find it here.

Tackling these kinds of subjects from the pulpit is not easy – it takes a degree of courage and sensitivity. But reluctance to risk such preaching can also be a result of simply not knowing how to go about it. What is offered here are some resources and ideas to assist the preacher.

The format is similar to that of the first book: a biblical text, some background information, sermon ideas, a story and a thought to take away. The authors bring their own expertise and particular style to that format.

About the contributors

RUPERT BRISTOW, a Reader in Trinity Benefice, Folkestone, is the author of six books of prayers and was Director of Education for Canterbury Diocese from 1995 until his retirement in 2008. He has taught on VSO, was the second Director of the UK Council for Overseas Student Affairs, and then Dean of Student Services at London South Bank University. He has also been a specialist adviser to a House of Commons Select Committee, edited and written for various educational publications and chaired Kent SACRE (Standing Advisory Council for Religious Education). He is an Honorary Fellow of Canterbury Christ Church University.

JOCELYN BRYAN is Director of Postgraduate Studies at the Wesley Study Centre and Cranmer Hall, St John's College, Durham. She is a Methodist local preacher and a member of the Faith and Order Committee of the Methodist Church. Her research interest is in the interface between psychology, theology and Christian ministry. She co-edited *The Christian Handbook of Abuse, Addiction and Difficult Behaviour* and contributed to the book *Sexual Issues: Understanding and Advising in a Christian Context*.

TONY CASTLE is a dispensed-to-marry Catholic priest, who, over the past 35 years, has worked in Catholic publishing and Catholic education. Since his retirement Tony has worked part-time as a school chaplain and as a diocesan inspector of schools. After initially writing to promote Catholic youth work in the 1970s, Tony's more recent publications – numbering over 50 – have been aids to school and parish worship. His best-known *Quotes and Anecdotes for Preachers and Teachers* has been in print for the last 30 years.

HELEN COSTIGANE is a member of the Society of the Holy Child Jesus. Holding degrees from the universities of Glasgow, London, and Leuven, she teaches Canon Law and Christian Ethics at Heythrop College, University of London.

JOHN COX recently retired as Diocesan Director of Education in the diocese of St Edmundsbury and Ipswich, where he had previously been Archdeacon of Sudbury. He served as a parish priest in Lancashire, Birmingham and London and for eight years was Director of Ordinands in the Diocese of Southwark. He now concentrates on school governorship, writing and editing. It doesn't leave him as much time for golf as he would like.

PAUL COX went into parish ministry in 1990, having been a teacher for 24 years, the last 10 of which he was chaplain and headmaster of a prep school. For the next 16 years he served in rural parishes in Canterbury Diocese. At various times, he was in addition part-time Director of Selection and Training for Readers, Bishop's Officer for NSMs and then OLMs. On retirement to Chichester Diocese he tutors on courses for the Bishop's Certificate and is an examining chaplain.

BRIAN FAHY was born in 1947 of Lancashire and Irish parentage. For many years he was a priest in a Catholic preaching order (Redemptorists). Now laicised and widowed, with one son, he is still writing homilies for publication – to dig he is not able – and also employed by Relationships Scotland as a family mediator, helping separating parents make good arrangements for their children. He is a lifelong supporter of Bolton Wanderers, and has a lifelong love of the West of Ireland.

BRENDAN GEARY is a Marist Brother and counselling psychologist (UK registered). He has worked as a teacher, retreat worker, lecturer and psychotherapist. He has worked in the United Kingdom, Cameroon, and the United States, and has published papers on sex offenders, counselling, and spirituality. He co-edited *The Christian Handbook of Abuse, Addiction and Difficult Behaviour*, which was published in 2008. He co-edited the following two books with Joanne Marie Greer: *Sexual issues: Understanding and advising in a Christian context* (2010) and *The dark night of the Catholic Church: Examining the child sexual abuse scandal* (2011).

ED HONE is a member of the Redemptorist missionary order and is based in Luxembourg where he is parish priest of the English-speaking Catholic community. He specialises in mission development, preaching, and creative liturgy. Currently Ed is studying for a Doctorate in Theology and Ministry at the University of Durham. He is the author of *Fit for Purpose: a Lenten course in spiritual health* (2012).

DEBORAH JONES grew up in the country, surrounded by animals, and is now part-time General Secretary of Catholic Concern for Animals, with a published doctoral thesis on the Catholic theology of animals. After university and teaching English and Classics, she was introduced to theology while with a Franciscan Order in Rome, and continued those studies in Cambridge and Wales. In 1980 Deborah was appointed Director of Adult Religious Education for the Diocese of East Anglia, and has served on the Bishops Conference Committees of Ministerial Formation and of Theology. She was also Editor of the Catholic Herald for two years. Deborah combines her work as a freelance journalist with sub-editing and homiletic writing.

BRUCE KENT has been active in the peace and justice world for over 50 years. He is currently a vice-president of Pax Christi, CND and the Movement for the Abolition of War. He is a past Chair of War on Want. He did his National Service in the Armoured Corps and then studied law before spending, prior to retirement, many years as a curate, parish priest and university chaplain in London.

ALISON MOORE currently works as Adviser in Pastoral Care and Counselling for the Diocese of Durham, Church of England. Alison was brought up in London, studied English Literature, and taught it in a secondary school. Later she started to work with adults instead of young people, in counselling and training, particularly specialising in work with conflicted relationships. She now runs the diocesan counselling service in Durham, as well as being involved in pastoral care training and consultancy for lay people and ministers. She contributed to *The Christian Handbook of Abuse, Addiction and Difficult Behaviour* and *Sexual Issues: Understanding and Advising in a Christian Context*. She is married with four adult sons and three grandsons.

CHRIS MORLEY worked for nearly 40 years as a Methodist minister, mostly in London. He was involved in school and prison chaplaincy as well as local church ministry. He enjoys the new insights that often come from applying the Christian message to contemporary issues. He retired in 2009, partly to be his wife's carer, but also to write. He is the author of *Caring Together*, a handbook for carers and all involved in caring; and *The Heart of Christmas* and *Tasting Life*, books of daily reflections for Advent and Lent respectively. His website is www.chrismorley.org

PAUL NICHOLSON is a Roman Catholic priest of the Society of Jesus (the Jesuits). He is currently responsible for the initial training of candidates from north-west Europe, in the Jesuit novitiate in Birmingham, England. Since ordination in 1978 he has worked in the fields of social justice, as a community development worker in Sunderland, and of spirituality, spending six years as Director of the Loyola Hall spirituality centre on Merseyside. He is editor of the British Jesuit spirituality journal *The Way*, and author of a practical guide to prayer techniques, *Growing into Silence*. He is passionately interested in medieval churches.

SIOBHÁN O'KEEFFE was born in Cork, Ireland, and is a Sister of the Sacred Hearts of Jesus and Mary (Chigwell Sisters). She is a registered general nurse with specialist interest in palliative and dementia care, she offers spirituality and dementia training in Ireland and the UK and works in community outreach programmes in Dagenham, Essex. Siobhán holds an MA in Applied Theology, Justice, Peace and Mission Studies from the Missionary Institute, London. She is the author of three books: *Petals of Prayer – Prayers and Reflections for people with dementia and their carers*; *Beloved of the Lord – Reflections and Resources for people with special needs and their carers*; and *A Time of Wonder – Daily reflections and prayers for Advent*. She enjoys reading, gardening, walking and music appreciation.

JOHN PARR is Director of Ministry, Education and Training in the Diocese of St Edmundsbury and Ipswich. He has been involved for many years in parish ministry, education and training in the church and the voluntary sector, and has a keen interest in mental health. His work with Bible Reading Fellowship and Roots has enabled him to make biblical scholarship more widely accessible.

ROBERT REISS is currently Canon Treasurer and Sub-Dean of Westminster Abbey, where he has recently completed a thesis on *The Testing of Vocation*, which covers the history of the Central Advisory Council for Training for the Ministry from its foundation in 1912 to the current Ministry Division of the Archbishops' Council. Prior to that he was Archdeacon of Surrey and before that Team Rector of Grantham.

CLARE RICHARDS is a retired religious education teacher and author of resource books for primary and secondary schools, including lives of the saints for children. Her most recent book is the biography of her late husband, the biblical scholar and theologian, Hubert Richards, who published many books with Kevin Mayhew. Clare has contributed articles in periodicals and papers over the years, and is a regular guest on local radio. Now a busy grandma, she still enjoys giving talks on scripture, working for Unicef, and enthusiastically supporting Norwich City Football Club.

EDGAR RUDDOCK is an Anglican priest, who worked as a parish priest in inner-city Birmingham for nine years before moving to Southern Africa in 1983. There, over nearly nine years, he was involved mainly in the training and formation of clergy and lay people, in the context of the struggle against apartheid. Returning to the UK in 1991, he became Rector of Stoke upon Trent. In 2003 he joined the staff of *USPG: Anglicans in World Mission* where he is a Deputy General Secretary, with responsibility for leadership development programmes. He is married with three children, and three grandchildren.

JOHN SAXBEE retired as Bishop of Lincoln in 2011. Born in Bristol, he studied at Bristol and Durham Universities. His doctoral research was on the writings of Soren Kierkegaard. He was ordained in 1972 and held parochial posts in Plymouth before being appointed Director of Training for the Diocese of Exeter and Joint Director of the South West Ministry Training Course. He was Bishop and Archdeacon of Ludlow for eight years before translation to Lincoln in 2001. His publications include *Liberal Evangelism* (SPCK 1994) and *No Faith in Religion* (O Books 2009). He reviews books on religion and philosophy for various journals.

RAY SIMPSON is a Celtic new monastic for tomorrow's world, a lecturer, consultant, liturgist, and author of some 30 books. He is the founding guardian of the international Community of Aidan and Hilda and the pioneer of its e-studies programmes. He is an ordained member of the Christian church and lives on the Holy Island of Lindisfarne. His website is www.raysimpson.org

JOY TETLEY was formerly Archdeacon of Worcester and is now focusing on a ministry of prayer, writing, teaching and counsel. She has served in ordained ministry for many years, being involved during this time in parish and cathedral ministry and various forms of theological education. She also has a keen interest in ecumenism and has been involved in a number of ecumenical dialogues. She has a special passion for the Bible and its relevance for today and has produced a number of publications in this area.

HELEN WARWICK is a spiritual director, writer and occupational therapist. She has had a healing journey through a chronic illness. She works with people individually and runs courses and retreats. Her passion is to help others with their journey through life using a creative approach. Her published books include *Creating Gardens in the Desert* and *Finding Your Inner Treasure.*

Abortion

Alison Moore

For it was you who formed my inward parts;
you knit me together in my mother's womb.
I praise you, for I am fearfully and wonderfully made.
Wonderful are your works; that I know very well.
My frame was not hidden from you,
when I was being made in secret,
intricately woven in the depths of the earth.

Psalm 139:13-15

Background information

Abortion, 'the expulsion of a foetus from the womb', is an event which can occur naturally, but deliberately-induced abortion has become something of a central issue in some Christian circles. Opinions about abortion are likely to be affected by where we live and what the legal status of abortion is there. Proportionately, there are many more abortions in the developing world than in developed countries, and of those, many are unsafe (i.e. carried out by someone who is unskilled in an unsuitable place).

Those countries which forbid or restrict abortion make it an unsafe procedure with serious consequences for the health of the mother. Where abortion is legally permitted, abortion is usually safe and rates are low. In the UK and USA, one in three women will have had an abortion by the time they are 45. In 2008, nearly 200,000 abortions were carried out in England and Wales, and 40,000 in Scotland. In Northern Ireland abortion remains illegal as the 1967 Abortion Act was not accepted there.

The Act allows for abortion up to 24 weeks, with the consent of two doctors. (Later abortions can only be carried out if there are severe abnormalities or risk.) Although the Act stipulates that the doctors should judge that there is greater risk in continuing the pregnancy than in terminating it, in practice the decision usually respects 'the woman's right to choose' in matters of her own reproductive health. While factual information about abortion is easily accessible, it is interesting, though unsurprising, that the language used is very different depending on whether the organisation is 'pro-choice' or 'pro-life'. The medical and reproductive health organisations use neutral and non-emotive language: 'pregnancy termination', 'procedures', 'abortion treatment options'. The pro-life organisations use the language of 'killing' and 'unborn child'.

Sermon ideas

Mention of abortion raises hackles and provokes righteous indignation on both sides of the debate, with both pro- and anti-abortionists claiming biblical validation for their points of view.

In the western world, at the heart of the anti-abortion standpoint is a deep respect for the sanctity of human life, an unarguably Christian view. Anti-abortionists, however, sometimes seem to respect the unborn foetus' right to life at the expense of the rights to life of others, for example those who hold different opinions or even the mother herself. On the other hand, those who support abortion have a deep respect for the right of the individual to make decisions about their own life, hence the mother's 'right to choose'. This too has its roots in the biblical tradition where, in both Old and New Testaments, the individual is valued regardless of his or her status or importance. Where the 'right to choose' group comes unstuck, however, is in ignoring the clear biblical themes of community life and loving mutual responsibility that mark God's people: an individual belongs within a web of relationships, not just to his or her biological mother.

The anxieties that underlie each position are understandable: in the developed world, the pro-lifers fear that the life of a new human being will be sacrificed to the superficial whim or convenience of a woman and her family. The pro-abortionists fear that the terrible pressures and oppression that women have experienced when pregnant and raising large families only increase where abortion is outlawed. Indeed the scapegoating, punishing and blaming of pregnant women, seen in many societies throughout the world and across the ages, has also been shamefully prevalent in Christian churches too. This is an irony for a religion with a young unmarried mother at the heart of its story, and a history of care for those who are vulnerable and rejected.

What we now know about the early development of the foetus in the womb confirms the lyrical poetry of Psalm 139, where the picture of the unborn child, already known and loved by God who 'knit me together in my mother's womb' suggests that we cannot simply dismiss 'it' as 'foetus' but need to marvel at him or her as 'baby'. This in itself does not lead to a clear answer to the ethical question of whether abortion is always 'right' or 'wrong'.

When we approach ethical dilemmas seeking the Christian view, there are two things to remember. First, the question for the Christians is not 'How can we get everyone to agree on this ethical issue?' but 'How can we live with mutual respect in the same church with Christians who have opposing views?' Second, pastoral and ethical responses are often different. The ethical makes a judgement about right and wrong; the pastoral makes no judgement, but comes alongside the person in need. The pro-life Christian accepts lovingly their friend who has had an abortion; the pro-choice Christian stands by their friend as they live through the birth and death of their damaged baby.

Story

Mary was a pregnant teenager. Like so many unmarried pregnant women in all societies and through all ages, she could have been rejected, even executed. Her family risked social shame by standing by her. Why didn't her mother take her for a local backstreet abortion?

Thought to take away

How do we live both ethically and pastorally? Do we love people whose opinions we cannot share? Do we take seriously Matthew 7:1, 2: 'Do not judge, so that you may not be judged. For with the judgement you make you will be judged, and the measure you give will be the measure you get.'

Abstinence

Ray Simpson

Don't you realise that in a race everyone runs, but only one person gets the prize? So run to win! All athletes are disciplined in their training. They do it to win a prize that will fade away, but we do it for an eternal prize. So I run with purpose in every step. I am not just shadow-boxing. I discipline my body like an athlete, training it to do what it should. Otherwise, I fear that after preaching to others I myself might be disqualified.

1 Corinthians 9:24-27 (New Living Translation – NLT)

Background information

Fasting is practised to varying degrees in all the monotheist faiths, who recognise that regular disciplines are necessary if their adherents, who are both physical and spiritual beings, are not to become flabby. Addiction to food, drugs, alcohol, sex, money and digital chatter has reached epidemic proportions in western countries. These addictions distort, diminish and destroy life. Organisations such as the National Audit Office and the UK Government Health Select Committee estimate that the costs of various forms of addiction are astronomical, whether in terms of reduced productivity, mortality, health care, welfare benefits and social exclusion.

So abstinence is a central issue. The point of abstinence is not to become a killjoy, it is to defeat addiction and to be fit for purpose.

Sermon ideas

The point of God's command to the first humans to abstain from eating from 'the tree of good and evil' (Genesis 2:16, 17) was to lead Adam, the progenitor of the human race, to recognise the necessary dependence of creature upon Creator. The Laws of Moses required the people of Israel to abstain from normal business one day in seven. In the creation story, God rested on the seventh day (the Sabbath) and a root meaning of the word Sabbath is 'to desist'. In times of need, leaders called the people to special days or weeks of fasting in order to seek God's help (for example, 1 Kings 21:12; 2 Chronicles 20:3; Nehemiah

9:1). In the New Testament, fasting is more often related to a need to clear the body and mind in order to overcome temptations and seek God. The point of Christ preparing for his public ministry with 40 days of fasting in a desert was to gain mastery of his inner demons before expending all his energies on bringing God's kingdom into the world. For the apostle Paul, in the Bible reading above, the point of abstinence is to be fit for purpose.

The fifth-century fathers and mothers of the desert became known as Athletes of Christ. Their two basic ideas were to master cravings by going without something for which they craved; and to undertake a spiritual exercise which increased in them the virtue which is the opposite of the vice. They used abstinence as a tool to overcome eight destructive tendencies: gluttony, love of money, anger, self-pity, lust, laziness, vanity and pride. Such abstinence is not an end in itself, it is so that we may express our love for the God of life.

Story

Sven Aasmundtveit was a couch potato. Until one summer's day, at the age of 30, he headed into a fjord in tiny swimming trunks and his wife remarked that he had 'spare tyres' round his abdomen. That brutal revelation marked a turning point. He started exercising. At first, he was exhausted after a few hundred metres.

But recognition of the harsh reality had begun. You need to start exercising! Sven said, 'I think it must have been the most miserable start of an athletic career. I ran a few hundred metres with the taste of blood in the mouth and shaky leg muscles.' He returned to his home at slow walking speed and the allure of the couch continued! But he persevered. The first week was terrible. The next month was not good. He set himself small goals along the way and was delighted when each of these goals was reached. Slowly but surely torture turned into the tolerable and eventually he felt really good!

Sven then realised that he needed training for his spiritual health, too – he had the spiritual equivalent of 'spare tyres'. He was a Lutheran pastor in Norway. He had confused the fact that every good thing we receive comes from God's grace with the idea that we ourselves can do nothing. He studied the fifth century desert fathers known as Athletes of Christ, engaged in spiritual disciplines, and learned to listen to horses. He created a training course entitled *Athletes of Christ: a handbook to a practical Christian life* (written in Norwegian). In this he likens the desert to a gym. It is necessary to abstain from alternative pleasures in order to make time for the gym, and in order to grow strong in virtues such as simplicity, purity and obedience. But the aim is not to prove something or be better than others. Those who join Sven's spiritual gym abstain from many false pursuits, but the measure of all things is love.

Thought to take away

It is necessary to break free from the grip of all things in order to love all.

Adoption

Helen Costigane

There is one Lord, one faith, one baptism, one God and Father of all, who is above all and through all and in all.

Ephesians 4:5, 6

Background information

Adoption is generally defined as a means of having children other than by natural generation. Married couples, single individuals and, more recently couples in same-sex relationships adopt not only babies, but often children who are considered harder to place, particularly those with physical disabilities or who suffer from emotional and psychological problems. The shortage of babies to adopt, and the often lengthy procedures involved in this country, sometimes causes individuals or couples to seek to adopt children from other countries.

Sermon ideas

Sometimes parents have to give up children for a number of reasons, including financial pressures, emotional distress, mental illness, or generally an inability to cope with a child. This can lead to a range of feelings in the years that follow, most often an unbearable sadness particularly around the date of the child's birthday. Sometimes, though, there is a degree of happiness that the right choice was made for the sake of the child. For adoptive parents, this 'chosen child' comes at a price. This is not just a financial one in terms of raising the child, but in a loss of privacy in having to have their lives scrutinised as they are assessed for their fitness to adopt. Giving a home to an older child who may come with their own set of problems may also entail a cost to the adoptive parents in terms of emotional support, patience and perseverance.

For the child who is adopted, there may be mixed emotions – gratitude to the birth mother for the gift of life and to the adoptive parents for the blessings of a loving home. At the same time, there may also be a sense of rejection in that the birth mother 'gave me away' and incompleteness in that 'I don't know where I came from'. When to inform a child that he or she is adopted remains a difficult issue. Some argue that it is better never to tell, though recent developments in being able to trace birth parents render this less of an option. More often than not, children will want to know where they come from. This is particularly true in an age when the question 'where do I come from?' has given rise to the hobby of tracing family ancestries and roots. The tracing of birth parents can give rise to the fear of rejection: by the child who may reject the parent who placed them for adoption, by the birth parent on being faced with the child they 'gave away', and by the adoptive parents by the child on finding their 'real parents'.

The issue of adoption raises the question as to what children owe their adoptive parents and, if they find them, their birth parents. The fourth commandment reminds us that we must honour our father and mother (Exodus 20:12). However, as it speaks about caring relationships, it need not be interpreted strictly as relating to biological parents. Rather, this text enjoins us to care and honour all of those who have parented us from childhood to interdependent adulthood, and who have given us love, patience, direction, and space to grow.

However, as it is often the case that adoption in human experience is most commonly seen as a remedy to a problem (for example, where a birth parent gives up a child through rejection or inadequacy, or a couple adopt because they cannot have children of their own), what does it mean that we are God's adopted sons and daughters? There are a number of references in St Paul's letters in the New Testament to God's adoption of us as his children (Romans 8:15; Galatians 4:5). This brings with it a call to love, kindness, and gentleness (Galatians 5:22). This gratitude to God, and the human response St Paul calls for, may serve as a model of thankfulness towards adoptive parents, and a model of forgiveness and acceptance – if needed – towards birth parents.

But it is more than this. God has chosen that we should *be* and he knew us before we were formed in the womb (Jeremiah 1:5). Further, he decided in advance to adopt us as his children (Ephesians 1:5), but what does this mean? It is not that he does this as some kind of remedy because we have been rejected by our birth parents, or because God cannot have more children. What this image of God tells us about is that God chooses us and makes us his sons and daughters. Rather than giving us a vague instinct that God loves us, this invitation to become God's 'chosen child' gives us a security in our relationship with him. This revelation of God's intentional love for us is clearly stated in a well-known verse in John's Gospel: 'For God so loved the world that he gave his only Son, so that everyone who believes in him may not perish but may have eternal life' (John 3:16).

Story

To mothers in my life,
even knowing about each other,
one hated the choice she made,
while the second chose to discover.
I didn't know my life would change
when it changed from arms who'd hold;
one brought me in this world to live
but the other gave me a home.[1]

The words of Suzanne Gomez's song encapsulate some of the feelings of birth and adoptive parents and adopted children. The birth parent mourns the fact that she has to give up her child; the adoptive parent makes a conscious choice. One creates life; another nurtures it. Yet, this human understanding of adoption is not the same as God's adoption of us. He both creates and nurtures us.

Thought to take away

How do I respond to the idea of being God's 'chosen child'?

1. 'The mothers in my life', © Copyright Suzanne Gomez (1998).

Aids / HIV

Brendan Geary

Blessed are those who mourn: they shall be comforted.

Matthew 5:4 (New Jerusalem Bible)

'Let the one among you who is guiltless be the first to throw a stone at her.' Then he bent down and continued writing on the ground. When they heard this they went away one by one, beginning with the eldest, until the last one had gone and Jesus was left alone with the woman, who remained in the middle. Jesus again straightened up and said, 'Woman, where are they? Has no one condemned you?' 'No one, sir,' she replied. 'Neither do I condemn you,' said Jesus. 'Go away, and from this moment sin no more.'

John 8:7-11 (New Jerusalem Bible)

Background information

Aids, properly known as 'acquired immune deficiency syndrome' was first identified as a medical syndrome in the United States in 1981. Aids is caused by the HIV virus (Human immunodeficiency virus). It was first diagnosed in young homosexual men, unfortunately leading to it being described as the 'gay plague'. Since that time the virus has spread across the world, and in developing countries, especially in sub-Saharan Africa, the majority of victims are heterosexual. According to The World Health Organisation over 30 million people have died from Aids-related illnesses over the past 30 years. In Africa there are an estimated 14 million who are orphans as a result of their parents' deaths from Aids. Over 40 per cent of all new infections worldwide involve young people who are over 15 years of age.

When Aids was first diagnosed it was considered to be fatal. With advances in medication and treatment it is now considered a chronic but manageable condition, and those with the virus can live a normal lifespan.[2] Early diagnosis can lead to longer life expectancy. In 2011 5,600 people in the UK were diagnosed with HIV.

Sermon ideas

When people think of Aids/HIV they probably first think of homosexuality, or sexual promiscuity. As such, it often brings with it more than a hint of moral judgement and censure. For some people it may elicit feelings of compassion towards those who have the diagnosis and who may be suffering in various ways.

Rather than move immediately to sexual behaviour and sexual ethics, it might be better to begin with the various losses that are part of the lives of those with Aids or the HIV virus. Jesus said, 'Blessed are those who mourn.' People with Aids/HIV immediately suffer a range of losses. As one person said, 'The future isn't what it used to be.' While new regimes of medication can enable people to live relatively normal lives – I am thinking of Lord Smith, the former Labour cabinet minister, who continued to contribute to society after contracting the virus – aspects of personal behaviour will change, and a healthy life is dependent on taking medications. For people in the developing world this can be challenging if not impossible, because of aspects of culture, and the conditions of life in the developing world, as well as for financial reasons.

People with Aids/HIV lose some personal privacy, as aspects of their sexual lives and behaviour are made public. At the very least they must discuss their lives with medical professionals. This can lead to feelings of guilt and shame.

Aids/HIV is also about sexual behaviour. One of the consequences of the pandemic is the need for honest discussion of human sexual behaviour. It is clear that many people do not accept – or do not live by – the moral standards of the Christian Churches. This challenges the Churches to communicate a positive message about human sexuality that emphasises responsibility and restraint, along with freedom and spontaneity in the area of human loving and sexual expression.

More than many other parts of life, sexual behaviour can lead to judgement and condemnation. The association of Aids/HIV with homosexuality and promiscuity has led to fears and avoidance. This can be seen in the film *Philadelphia*, where the lawyer played by Denzel Washington moves from a certain amount of disgust and distancing, to involvement and compassion. Those who have met or worked with people who have the virus have undertaken a similar journey.

People in the Aids/HIV community taught us all a valuable lesson when someone with the syndrome said 'I am not dying of Aids: I am living with Aids.' The gospel calls us to life, no matter what personal circumstances we find ourselves in.

Jesus makes it clear in St John's Gospel, in the story of the woman taken in adultery (John 8:1-11), that none of us is in a position to cast stones at other people, particularly when it comes to the area of sexual behaviour. Jesus' compassionate stance is a model of how to respond to people who have the virus or the syndrome.

Story

Princess Diana is remembered for many reasons. Perhaps one of her more important gifts to society was her involvement and compassion towards people with Aids/HIV. Many people have seen the photograph of her holding hands with a person dying of Aids, and will remember the look of compassion in her eyes. Her simple gesture of humanity profoundly influenced people who thought differently of people who, until then, had been treated by many as 'untouchable.'

Thought to take away

It is easy to take a judgemental stance towards people whose sexual behaviour has resulted in them contracting Aids/HIV. We must remember that many people, like the tennis player Arthur Ashe, contracted the virus innocently. Many children were also born with the virus. The illness challenges us to respond with compassion and empathy to those who suffer, and to find ways to communicate our values in the area of sexuality in such a way that they are seen as a healthy and life-giving way to live our lives. Jesus told his followers: 'Blessed are the merciful: they shall have mercy shown them' (Matthew 5:7, New Jerusalem Bible). Aids/HIV is a call to mercy and understanding.

2. Key facts about HIV and Aids. Body and Soul, *The Times*, Tuesday, 3 July 2012, p.7.

Ambition

John Cox

Do nothing from selfish ambition or conceit, but in humility regard others as better than yourselves. Let each of you look not to your own interests, but to the interests of others.

Philippians 2:3, 4

Background information

Ambition is a powerful motivator. It provides one of the drives for achievement – either personal achievement or the achievement of another person or group one is emotionally attached to. Thus a child can be ambitious to be best in their class at a certain subject and this can be supported by the ambition of the parents for the child to be successful. As a positive motivator it directs effort towards a chosen aim, the achievement of which enhances a sense of worth. The target to be achieved may be privately or publically known.

But there is an ambivalence about ambition. It has a good and a bad face. At its worst it can lead to obsessive behaviour and a determination to succeed *at all costs.* It can thus result in a disregard of other people who may be viewed as 'getting in the way' or to dishonest behaviour, from simple cheating to criminal activity.

The young Rory McIlroy had the ambition to become the greatest golfer in the world. With the support of his parents, and a great deal of talent, he achieved this in the spring of 2012 when he reached the position of number one golfer, the second youngest person ever to do so. In all this he retained a charm and pleasant personality that endeared him to thousands of fans across the world.

The ambition to be the leader of the greatest nation in the world, proving its supremacy by the domination of others led Adolf Hitler to plunge the world into six years of war and the deaths of millions.

Sermon ideas

In writing to the church at Philippi, St Paul appears to have made a distinction between ambition and selfish ambition. It is the latter that he warns against. Such ambition seeks to gain personal aggrandisement as a way of boosting one's own position over that of others. It is a matter of conceit that raises one's own sense of worth at the cost of belittling others. For Paul the Christian attitude should be one of humility with a sense of the needs and interests of others as a top priority. The person who climbs the greasy pole of success by clambering all over others is not following in the way of Jesus.

The sons of Zebedee, James and John were not without ambition. They wanted Jesus to promise them top places in his coming kingdom. St Matthew suggests that it was their mother's ambition for them that led to the request. Either way Jesus gave them little encouragement. To follow him to glory they would have to endure what he would have to endure ('drink the cup I drink') and in any case seating arrangements in the kingdom of God were not his responsibility. The account in Mark's Gospel shows that inappropriate ambition can have consequences for relationships with others. When they heard what John and James had been up to the other disciples became angry, no doubt in part out of jealousy. Jesus took the opportunity to give them all a lesson in what the true ambition of a disciple should be – not to lord it over others but to serve others (Mark 10:41-46).

But not all ambition is wrong or inappropriate. Indeed without some kind of ambition there would be little progress in personal or national life. Jesus' view seems to make the necessary distinction between the ambition that encourages one's gifts and efforts into self-importance and the ambition that encourages one's gifts and efforts into the service of others. Such service might come from positions that are comparatively humble, with little public recognition. But positions of eminence do not in themselves show that a person has been wrongly ambitious. To use the gifts and talents that God has given you to the very best of your ability may mean that you achieve a position of considerable prestige and responsibility, power even. It is how you use that position that matters – for the good of others or for selfish ends. Retaining the stance of a servant while occupying a position of eminence takes a mature personality and spirituality.

Among those who are ordained the question of ambition is always tricky. It is so difficult to retain the delicate balance between personal prestige and public service. Being such a delicate balance leads some to condemn any form of ambition. Better to have no ambition than to get it wrong. But that is spiritual cowardice. There should be ambition for the gospel, ambition for the kingdom, ambition to nourish people in the faith, ambition to care for others after the pattern of Jesus. And to do so in the most effective way possible. If that means being an archdeacon or a cardinal, a superintendent or a district chairman, so be it, so long as the position is for the service of others. Only then can it be the place where God wants the person to be.

In directing the Philippians' attention to Jesus, Paul went on to say this: 'Let the same mind be in you that was in Christ Jesus, who, though he was in the form of God, did not regard equality with God as something to be exploited, but emptied himself, taking the form of a slave, being born in human likeness. And being found in human form, he humbled himself and became obedient to the point of death – even death on a cross (Philippians 2:5-8). The ambition to follow in the way of Christ can lead to a glory that is only discovered in humility.

Story

The two brothers could hardly have been more different. As a child Edgar was into fighting and playing soldiers, while Stephen went birdwatching and took home armfuls of wild flowers for his mum. Edgar had no doubt about what he wanted to do. Asked what he would be when he grew up he would always answer, 'A captain of industry' although he had little idea what it actually entailed. Stephen wanted to be a shepherd. Edgar retired as managing director of a major company, with a reputation for being ruthless. Those who went to his retirement 'do' went out of duty, not affection. Stephen never retired. He died of a heart attack tending a ewe as she lambed. The whole village went to his funeral and wept for the shepherd of the best flock in the county.

Thought to take away

Without ambition we will achieve little that is of worth either to ourselves or to others. With nothing but ambition we may achieve a lot but at a cost that is too high for our own good or for the well-being of others.

Anger

Helen Warwick

One who is slow to anger is better than the mighty, and one whose temper is controlled than one who captures a city.

Proverbs 16:32

Background information

Anger is a natural human emotion that is often misunderstood. Society imparts mixed messages about anger; when children are small tantrums are acceptable, but from age 5 or so they are criticised. Some of the teachings in churches can give the impression that anger is a sin and it is wrong to feel or express this emotion.

Anger can be aroused when a person perceives that he or she is threatened, rejected, put down, ignored or humiliated. It often follows hurt. Human anger is harmful when expressed for self-centred motives, wanting revenge. It is frequently condemned in the Bible, as a person who is angry can become blinkered and violent.

Anger can also be aroused at the injustices in the world. The energy that anger has can be a motivational force for bringing God's justice in the world. However, many people do not acknowledge their anger so it is often suppressed, leading to mental, physical and emotional problems.

Sermon ideas

It is reasonable to be angry.

We are made in God's image and there are many instances of God's anger in the Bible. Isaiah paints a vivid description of this anger in chapter 30:27-33. In Exodus God is furious when the Israelites turn to idol worship and build a golden calf (32:9, 10), but his anger is also aroused through his compassion when widows and orphans are ill-treated and they cry out to him (22:22-24). King Saul's anger was kindled through the spirit of God that came upon him when he was told that the Ammonites had threatened his people (1 Samuel 11:6).

Suppressed anger

It is helpful to recognise and connect to the emotion of inner anger, although some people are frightened by this thought. Suppressed anger can destroy peace of mind and eat away at the immune system. It will express itself in mental and physical problems such as grinding teeth, tensions, excessive irritability, vivid dreams, stomach ulcers and depression. Many people will be able to find some hidden anger within them and observing thoughts can assist with this recognition. Reflecting on situations and relationships can help find the roots to this emotion. The tensions in the body may also be linked to these thoughts. If anger is unrecognised or not expressed safely then it may also lead to damaging other humans. Paul tells the Ephesians not to sin in their anger and not to let the sun go down on their anger, which would give the devil a foothold (Ephesians 4:26, 27).

Bring your emotions to God

God understands our feelings, and it is only in the expression of honest feelings that there can be a connection with God in intimate ways. Discharging anger is helpful if there is a language that it can speak through, for example speaking it out, splashing colour on paper, clay work or physical movement, such as hitting safe objects. Writing a letter to God expressing feelings and then destroying the letter can purge anger.

Controlling anger

Once anger is recognised and acknowledged there are helpful ways of bringing it under control. Counting to ten before speaking, calming the breath and avoiding ruminating on negative thoughts can help. James advises – 'everyone should be quick to listen, slow to speak and slow to become angry, for man's anger does not bring about the righteous life that God desires' (James 1:19, 20, NIV). Learning to re-evaluate situations and being assertive, rather than aggressive, can also assist. For those whose anger is a problem there are anger management courses available on the NHS.

Anger can be controlled but it does take strength of mind. In the opening Bible verse Solomon wrote that a man who controls his temper is more worthy than a warrior who captures a city.

Use anger as a gift

Anger has great energy. Often work on suppressed anger can release this energy. This can be used in a constructive way to bring about God's justice in the world. Constructive anger can be life-giving, assisting in setting personal boundaries, defending from harm, and helping to establish individuality; to notice what we are passionate about and how we can help change the world for good.

Story

Freud once likened anger to the smoke in an old-fashioned wood-burning stove. The normal avenue for the discharge of the smoke is up the chimney – a safe outlet that is built for that purpose. If the normal avenue is blocked, the smoke will leak out of the stove in unintended ways, around the door, through the grates for example, choking everyone in the room. If all avenues of escape are blocked, the fire goes out and the stove ceases to function.

Thought to take away

Destructive anger is the repression of feelings, dampening the fire and inhibiting healing.

Take time to tend to your stove, making sure you have a good outlet for any angry smoke. Use the flame to burn for good causes.

Animal rights

John Saxbee

God created human beings in his own image; in the image of God he created them; male and female he created them. God blessed them and said to them, 'be fruitful and increase, fill the earth and subdue it, have dominion over the fish in the sea, the birds of the air, and every living thing that moves on the earth'.

Genesis 1:27, 28 (Revised English Bible)

Background information

One well-known dictionary lists Anglicans between angels and animals – and it is not only Anglicans who would be quite content to think of themselves in that way. Most people would gladly think of themselves as a bit lower than the angels and a good bit above members of the animal kingdom. But perhaps we ought to think twice before taking it for granted that this is an appropriate way to prioritise beings in God's creation. Maybe we are too quick to classify living creatures and place them in a hierarchy of value and worth. After all, distinctions between angels, animals and humans are often blurred. We habitually describe sweet young children or devoted nurses as 'angels' whilst it was a human being who ended up being described as the Beast of Belsen. We should be especially cautious about invoking a hierarchy of beings when it comes to attributing or withholding rights – and particularly when it comes to promoting and defending the rights of animals.

Sermon ideas

On the face of it, the Bible gives us the right to confer rights on other creatures – or to withhold them. After all, doesn't the Creation story in Genesis tell us that God has given human beings dominion over all other creatures? This has been taken to mean that we are superior to animals just as angels are superior to us. We have been given authority to treat animals as at our disposal and there is plenty of evidence to suggest that human beings have taken this very literally over the centuries. A recent estimate indicates that some 25 billion animals are slaughtered for human use every year.

But it is by no means clear that we have interpreted that text correctly. Most commentators would see it as the conferring of an obligation to be good stewards of God's creation. We have been charged with respecting and protecting other creatures rather than being given a mandate to subjugate and exploit them. Whilst Jesus had little or nothing to say specifically about animal rights, he does make a clear distinction between good and bad shepherds – and identifies himself with those who know their sheep, care for them and protect them.

So when we talk about animal rights we could do worse than think of them as having an absolute right to our protection. For some people, that will mean becoming vegetarians or getting active in an anti-vivisection movement. For others, it will be sufficient to ensure the best possible welfare for animals at abbatoirs and in laboratories where it is shown beyond doubt that experiments on animals are absolutely necessary for the common good. But an animal's right to human protection will almost certainly call into question hunting them for sport or using them in the development of cosmetics.

Angels, animals – and even Anglicans! – are all part of God's creation, and how we treat animals will be a key test of our humanity.

Story

Laurens van der Post has told of a female ostrich, surprised with her mate by his truck's sudden arrival over a ridge of the desert:

'Knowing how ostriches hate and fear men, I do not think I have ever seen a braver deed. The bird was desperately afraid. Her heart beating visibly in her throat, she advanced towards us like a soldier against a machine-gun post. With the afternoon sun making a halo round her feathers, she came on pretending to be mortally hurt, limping badly and trailing one wing as if it were broken . . . Meanwhile the male hurried the other way in a zigzag fashion like a ship tacking into the wind . . . When his rushes had presently taken him into a bare patch of sand higher up on the ridge, we saw the cause of it all: the male was trying to hustle out of danger nineteen little ostrich chickens, while the female distracted our attention by doing all she could to entice us into capturing her instead.'[3]

Thought to take away

The ostrich is prepared to sacrifice herself to protect her vulnerable young, just as Jesus the Lamb of God was prepared to sacrifice himself for our sake. The extent to which we in our turn are prepared to sacrifice our own interests for the sake of creatures entrusted to our care may well be evidence not only of our humanity, but also of the divine spark which is within us as children of God.

---

3. Laurens van der Post, *The Heart of the Hunter*, Hogarth Press, 1961. pp.99, 100.

Anti-Semitism

Edgar Ruddock

Why do you see the speck in your neighbour's eye, but do not notice the log in your own eye? Or how can you say to your neighbour, 'Friend, let me take out the speck in your eye', when you yourself do not see the log in your own eye? You hypocrite, first take the log out of your own eye, and then you will see clearly to take the speck out of your neighbour's eye.

Luke 6:41, 42

Background information

Christians cannot begin to think sensibly or seriously about anti-Semitism unless they are first willing to acknowledge the sins and failings of our Christian forebears, and by cultural and religious inheritance, our own implicit involvement.

Two key things fed Christian antipathy to Judaism: one was the New Testament teaching that it was the Jews who were responsible for the death of Jesus; the other was the persecution of Christians by Jews who saw this sect breaking away from, and challenging the fundamentals of their own deeply held beliefs.

These fears and growing hatreds – which run quite counter to the teaching of Jesus himself – were reinforced by the apparent separateness of Jewish communities around the diaspora (the Jewish communities scattered around Europe and Asia as a result of the destruction of Jerusalem in AD60). Later this was fuelled by their increasing economic success, which led to all manner of jealousies and rivalries down to the present day.

Sermon ideas

We have much for which to be thankful in our Jewish inheritance!

- Our belief in a personal God who reveals himself in relational terms comes from the Jewish understanding of the divine.
- From that we derive a sense of the wholeness of our humanity – very close to Jesus' heart – and somewhat in contrast to Paul's more Greek understanding of the divide between body and spirit.
- From it we also receive the idea of the divine covenant – God's commitment to us, which carries

with it the call to respond to God, and to take responsibility with God for the world around us.
- From our Jewish roots we also receive the wonderful challenge to care for the marginalised, and the alien (or anyone different) in our society.

How do we as Christians tackle anti-Semitism?

- We have to recognise our complicity in the history of suffering of the Jewish people: even today, stereotypes in the media, talk in the pubs, and backchat in the schoolyards have done nothing to ease this blight of racial and religious hatred of one of the oldest religious and national communities on earth.
- In terms of the present conflict in the Middle East, we need to distinguish carefully between faith and nation state. Christians during the troubles in Ireland or in apartheid South Africa, have had to learn the hard way that we cannot link any idea of being chosen by God to claiming rights to land. Jesus was very clear that God's kingdom was not about land and power, or about ownership at the expense of others.
- We should not be afraid, while looking carefully into our own mistakes as Christians, to challenge the state of Israel over its policies towards the Palestinians, where it seems so often the Zionist State is meting out to others the very things it knows its own people have suffered from for generations. Justice and peace will only be found where the reconciling love of Christ is able to lead people to overcome the bondage and barriers of history.

Story

For years Grandma grumbled that her family kept trying to cheer her up, when there was little left to live for. They kept pointing out the beautiful things in the garden, or along the road as the car sped through the country. Their cheerfulness made her more and more depressed, and she constantly blamed them, and accused them of lying, when all around her she saw drabness, greyness, and confusion.

Then one day the doctor asked when her eyes were last tested. An examination showed cataracts in both eyes. The now simple operation was offered and grudgingly accepted, Grandma still fearing more do-goodism, and attempts to cheer her up.

Then suddenly she could see! Everything came into focus – a world full of colour and delight again – so much she had forgotten. It would be a long road to restore all those battered relationships – but now, as the world sparkled, Grandma began the long road back.

Thought to take away

It is all too easy to criticise others while not recognising what is wrong with our own lives and attitudes. This is a lesson that both Christians and Jews need constantly to re-learn. Getting rid of the beams in our own eyes will allow us to see the world more clearly as God sees it, to overcome our prejudices, and yet to be crystal clear, with our new improved eyesight, of the high calling of God's justice, which leads ultimately to reconciliation and peace.

Astrology

Ed Hone

Therefore do not worry, saying, 'What will we eat?' or 'What will we drink?' or 'What will we wear?' For it is the Gentiles who strive for all these things; and indeed your heavenly Father knows that you need all these things. But strive first for the kingdom of God and his righteousness, and all these things will be given to you as well. So do not worry about tomorrow, for tomorrow will bring worries of its own. Today's trouble is enough for today.

Matthew 6:31-34

Background information

Astrology supposes that the future of human beings, and indeed of nations, is literally 'written in the stars'. Millions of people check their horoscopes regularly, for fun or on a more serious basis. For thousands of years, as far back as the civilisation of Ancient Egypt, there has been a desire on the part of many to know what the future holds. There is, too, the feeling that knowing the future can allow one to influence it. How true this actually is, no one really knows.

Sermon ideas

Astrology can be a hot potato for Christians, some believing that it is nothing more than harmless fun or misguided thinking, whilst others believe it to be the work of the devil. But one thing that Christians will agree on is that astrology is *not* the Christian way. Christians do not believe in fate, where the future is mapped out and can therefore be read: people have free will, and can change the course of their lives and even the course of history by exercising that God-given free will. Underlying astrology is a sense of insecurity, a fear that all might not be well, and that knowing what is going to happen will equip us in some way to face it when it happens. If we imagine we can somehow change what is predicted, we could tie ourselves in mental knots trying to work out how a future 'written in the stars' can be altered!

Jesus offers an entirely different way of looking at the world. He points out to his listeners that the birds of the air are fed by God, even though they do not sow, reap or gather into barns; the lilies of the field, he adds, are clothed in greater riches than King Solomon even though they neither toil nor spin (Matthew 6:26-28). Here is a pointer to the disciple's way of life. In the verses that follow, Jesus describes discipleship in terms of a radical dependence on God, our heavenly Father – something entirely different from the negotiation of a mapped-out, arbitrary fate.

What of the three astrologers in the Gospel of Matthew? At first sight, Matthew's account of the wise men following the star to find the infant Jesus might seem like an endorsement of astrology, but in context what is happening is more profound. Just as Christians believe that the Jewish prophecies concerning the coming of the Messiah pointed towards Jesus, Matthew believes that the star-following of the wise men also points them to Christ. Paying homage to Jesus, they return home, being saved from falling into Herod's clutches by a God-sent dream. They had shown that the birth of the Christ-child was of significance not only to the Jewish people, but to the Gentile world too. In the Gospel of John, the miracles of Jesus are referred to as 'signs' – signs that he was the Messiah, and that the kingdom of God was at hand. But something else was, and is, true: Jesus himself was *the* sign of the saving presence of God. It is to the Lord that Christians look for guidance, reassurance and hope. Other signs are false and obscure the truth.

The wisest Christian response to astrology is to ignore it, not paying it the attention it doesn't deserve. Christians rely on God's providence; Christians believe in the power of prayer to change events, according to God's will; Christians believe that 'all things work together for good for those who love God' (Romans 8:28); Christians do not need to second-guess God, because we trust God will complete all things in Christ.

Story

Michel de Nostredame, or Nostradamus, was born in 1503 and rose to fame for publishing his prophecies which to this day are claimed by believers to predict world events. They have much in common with popular astrological predictions in that they are a study in ambiguity. The reader can see in the prophecies almost anything they wish. One celebrated example has Le Pelletier foreseeing a battle in which Napoleon was either victorious or was defeated.

When Napoleon was in fact defeated three years later in battle, Le Pelletier claimed the prophecy had come true![4]

Thought to take away

'When people stop believing in God, they don't believe in nothing – they believe in anything.'[5] Often people who believe religion to be irrational hold instead far less rational beliefs.

---

4. Edgar Leoni, *Nostradamus and his prophecies*, New York: Bell Publishing Company, 1982. pp.702-704. Quoted in http://en.wikipedia.org/wiki/Nostradamus#Alternative_views. Accessed 30 July 2012.
5. Popularly attributed to G. K. Chesterton; whilst not necessarily literally true, these words are often borne out.

Capitalism

Paul Cox

For what is a man profited, if he shall gain the whole world, and lose his own soul? Or what shall a man give in exchange for his soul?

Matthew 16:26 (King James Version)

Background information

Capitalism organises surplus money, wealth or savings, so that it can be economically productive. Out of this productivity it is expected that there should be surplus revenue over costs. This gain is called profit and is shared by those who originally risked their savings in the new productive venture. The system has raised the living standards of individuals and nations over several hundreds of years. It led to the industrialisation of Britain with such proponents as Adam Smith in his book *The Wealth of Nations* (published 1776). But alongside the great wealth that capitalism generated there was also the creation of a new class divide between the capitalist rich and the exploited labour force of industry. This led to capitalism being challenged by such people as Marx (the communist manifesto, 1846), suggesting alternative systems as exemplified later by the former Soviet Union, and still today in Cuba and China. Such alternative systems are based upon detailed controlled planning of production and consumption and have depended upon strong political leaders, resulting in dictatorships. Russia, since the break-up of the Soviet Union, and increasingly China, with its recent rapid economic growth, have been applying some of the ideas of capitalism. But the continued inequalities in the distribution of wealth that have dogged both of these major systems remain. It seems that only through a sophisticated democratic political system can the greater wealth created by capitalism be more fairly distributed, but even so the USA is evidence of persistent inequality.

Even in Britain, with its long history of democracy and political controls, weaknesses in the economic system can occur. The 2008 banking crisis, which was worldwide due to the global nature of huge banks, was a clear and painful reminder that the profit motive in capitalism can be the source of considerable threat to the system as well as being a benevolent sponsor of economic growth. Not only has it been a threat to the system but also to the livelihoods of many people innocent of causing the problem, yet who see only limited redress made by those responsible.

Investment, which creates the productive use of surplus holdings of money, does not just apply to industrial plant or national infra-structure. It can also be applied to people. The education system of a nation does just that with a high expectation of return for both individuals and the nation. Give a starving man a fish and he is fed for a day. Show the man how to make a net and fish for himself and he will be fed for a lifetime. But the man needs to eat while he is learning how to make and use a fishing net – that is someone's cost of such investment and a repayment will be expected. Such payment could be a fixed sum (a fee for the lesson) or could be a tax (for state education) or sharing of the new production of the fisherman – profit-sharing.

Sermon ideas

The Bible does not use the word 'profit' in the sense it is used when we think of capitalism, rather it mainly means 'gain or benefit', for capitalism had not been devised during biblical times. But this does not mean that the Bible has nothing to guide us in how we implement such a system. The quotation from Matthew points us to a very basic principle, that of prioritising our lives. For what personal gain do we strive?

The Christian faith starts with the basic premise that all of creation is a gracious act. It is a gift which God, out of love, wishes to share with us. Out of this self-giving love we have been granted a certain amount of control, which means that we can be productive by using the resources of the world. This leads to teaching about stewardship to guide us in our attitudes towards such productivity. In a strictly Christian economic system there would be mutual agreement about the production of goods and services, how they would be produced and how distributed. Meeting needs rather than making a profit would be the greater motivator. We can see this in action in the early Church: 'All who believed were together and had all things in common; they would sell their possessions and goods and distribute the proceeds to all, as any had need' (Acts 2:44, 45, also Acts 4:32-35). Love rather than profit, the joy of giving rather than personal gain, were the driving forces in their economic life.

But economies become more complicated than the small church communities of the time of St Paul. Caritas, the unselfish, non self-centred love that has to be dominant for the early Church's model to work, has not been evident even within Christian society over the last two thousand years. Human frailty, sinfulness, has meant that love directed in other directions has prevailed. 'The love of money is the root of all evil.' Some see the Church's role today as not so much speaking out against the system of capitalism as a whole, but rather denouncing where capitalism goes against the good of all. So it opposes both an extreme range in the holding of wealth as well as a failure to distribute the benefits of capitalism fairly. Exploitation of workers or threats to livelihoods by greed or irresponsible actions of others need to be exposed and challenged. It encourages ways by which wealth can be managed, surpluses invested and profits shared to help improve the living standards of all.

Story

It was a small community, a mission school. To it came an economics graduate, Stephen, who had learnt all about the benefits of the capitalist system, about wages paid according to productivity, about profits that enabled even more investment and increased standards of living. He learnt that the school's income largely depended upon how many students it attracted. So he expected the more experienced, 'better' teachers would be paid more. The school had a happy, purposeful feel. It looked as if it was thriving. The head teacher clearly played a significant part in leading such a successful school. At the end of the month Stephen went to the school office to collect his pay. As a newly graduated teacher he was surprised at the amount he was given. Was the school really that wealthy? If he was getting this much, the head must be receiving a very large salary, and this was meant to be a Christian school. Stephen expressed his concern and was gently told that every teacher received the same pay, including the head. 'We are paid for what we need, what we do is our gift in God's service, each according to our abilities.' It certainly made that young graduate reconsider his plan to return to England to get a higher-paid job.

Thought to take away

Jesus did not speak against money or wealth but rather warned against sinful attitudes and their resultant actions. Perhaps in the parable of the house builders he was also asking us to consider how we deal with risk taking.

Censorship

Paul Nicholson

We who are strong ought to put up with the failings of the weak, and not to please ourselves. Each of us must please our neighbour for the good purpose of building up the neighbour. For Christ did not please himself; but, as it is written, 'The insults of those who insult you have fallen on me.'

Romans 15:1-3

Background information

In 1559 the Vatican issued its first list of prohibited books. Over the next four centuries this was regularly updated, and was only finally abolished in 1966. Today the debate on censorship focuses particularly (although not exclusively) on material available online through the World Wide Web. It is widely reported that North Korea only allows its citizens access to three websites, while parents' attempts to control what their children have access to may well be defeated by the greater technological know-how of the younger generation. The United Kingdom has had a Freedom of Information Act since 2000. This currently generates some 120,000 requests for information each year; one in five of these is refused.

Sermon ideas

Jesus can at times seem like a fervent advocate of freedom of information. 'What you hear whispered, proclaim from the housetops' (Matthew 10:27). 'Nothing is hidden that will not be disclosed' (Luke 8:17). Taking passages like these, there would seem to be little scriptural warrant for any form of censorship. Yet in other situations, he appears equally anxious to control who knows what. In Mark's Gospel, his closest disciples are repeatedly instructed to tell no one what they have seen and heard. In Matthew, the crowds have to be content with parables; only the inner circle have the full meaning of these explained to them.

We might conclude from this a presumption of openness on the part of Christians, unless there are compelling reasons to withhold information. The above quotation from Romans would fit with this view, and yet offers one such compelling reason for restraint. The strong should allow their freedom to be restricted in order to protect those who are weaker. Such an idea lies at the heart of contemporary debates about censorship.

There are areas of our experience where such a stance is relatively uncontroversial. That children should be prevented from accessing hard-core pornography on the internet is a position that few would oppose. Most would agree that such access can be harmful, and that children themselves are not in the best position to judge the effect that this is likely to have on them. The advisability of banning adults from such access is more debatable. And when it comes to censoring less obviously harmful material, such as a government's reasons for going to war, opposition to the censor is likely to be greater.

Censorship involves balancing two goods that are sometimes in opposition to each other. It is normally good that people are protected from harm, including harmful written or visual material. It is also generally good that information is freely available, and not restricted to self-interested cabals. The decision of whether and what to censor involves weighing up the competing claims of these goods, and different individuals are likely to come to different judgements here. It is certainly not obvious that the value of freely available information should win out in every possible case.

Story

Oliver Wendell Holmes Jr was a Justice in the United States Supreme Court during the first three decades of the twentieth century. In a case involving the right to oppose conscription during World War I, he ruled that 'The most stringent protection of free speech would not protect a man falsely shouting fire in a theatre and causing a panic.' This image has entered popular culture as a demonstration of the acceptability of censorship, at least in times of, in another phrase from the same judgement by Holmes, 'clear and present danger'.

Thought to take away

There is a presumption in censorship that the one carrying out the censoring is immune from the harmful effects expected in the one being protected by the censorship. Maybe the censor has the appropriate security clearance; or is an adult acting to protect a juvenile; or simply assumes a position of moral superiority. It is worth asking, when it is proposed to censor anything, how far this presumption is justified. If I judge that I can approach this material without being adversely affected by it, what grounds do I have for thinking that it will harm you?

Childlessness

John Parr

There was a certain man of Ramathaim, a Zuphite from the hill country of Ephraim, whose name was Elkanah son of Jeroham son of Elihu son of Tohu son of Zuph, an Ephraimite. He had two wives; the name of one was Hannah, and the name of the other Peninnah. Peninnah had children, but Hannah had no children.

Now this man used to go up year by year from his town to worship and to sacrifice to the Lord of hosts at Shiloh. After they had eaten and drunk at Shiloh, Hannah rose and presented herself before the Lord. Now Eli the priest was sitting on the seat beside the doorpost of the temple of the Lord. She was deeply distressed and prayed to the Lord, and wept bitterly. She made this vow: 'O Lord of hosts, if only you will look on the misery of your servant, and remember me, and not forget your servant, but will give to your servant a male child, then I will set him before you as a nazirite until the day of his death. He shall drink neither wine nor intoxicants and no razor shall touch his head.'

Then Eli answered, 'Go in peace; the God of Israel grant the petition you have made to him.' And she said, 'Let your servant find favour in your sight.' Then the woman went to her quarters, ate and drank with her husband, and her countenance was sad no longer.

They rose early in the morning and worshipped before the Lord; then they went back to their house at Ramah. Elkanah knew his wife Hannah, and the Lord remembered her. In due time Hannah conceived and bore a son. She named him Samuel, for she said, 'I have asked him of the Lord.'

1 Samuel 1:1-3, 9-11, 17-20

Background information

Reasons for childlessness vary. A couple may have no children because they have chosen not to have them. Both may have demanding careers that leave them little time or energy for family life. One or both may believe that they lack the necessary parental 'instinct'. Or there may be a risk that their child will have a genetic disorder. A couple may be childless because one (or perhaps both) is infertile. They may seek to remedy the situation artificially, by *in vitro* fertilisation (which occurs outside the body) or artificial insemination (where fertilisation occurs within a woman's body but without sexual intercourse). In either case the sperm or eggs may belong to someone outside the relationship, necessarily so where the childless couple are gay or lesbian. Alternatively the couple, whether heterosexual or homosexual, may decide to adopt a child.

The vast majority of people are fertile at some time of life. To expect to be able to have children is natural, and reinforced from an early age by countless role models. To be infertile can bring shock, disappointment, grief, anger, shame and isolation. A recent study shows that women who remain childless after treatment for infertility are more likely to experience mental ill-health.[6] Those who believe that God's purpose is expressed in the command to 'be fruitful and multiply' (Genesis 1:28) may find childlessness particularly challenging.

Sermon ideas

To suggest that Elkanah and Hannah are simply childless would allow either or both to be considered infertile. Yet like other biblical women in similar circumstances, Hannah is the one who is stigmatised as barren: 'the Lord had closed her womb' (1 Samuel 1:2, 5). Her plight is aggravated by the provocations of Elkanah's other wife, Peninnah, who has children (1 Samuel 1:6). The men in the story only make matters worse. Elkanah lacks empathy (1 Samuel 1:8), and the priest Eli completely misunderstands Hannah's prayer of distress (1 Samuel 1:14).

Attitudes in our own day are informed by a culture of rights and consumer choice. Because most couples who want to can have children, it is easy to assume that fertility is a right that extends to all. When our identity is so bound up with exercising choice, not being able to choose in such a vital area can be understandably devastating.

In the biblical stories of women like Hannah, divine intervention comes to the rescue, and remedies what is essentially seen as a female problem. A more compassionate and prophetic response is found in Jesus' words to the women of Jerusalem on the Via Dolorosa. 'Daughters of Jerusalem, do not weep for me, but weep for yourselves and your children. For the days are surely coming when they will say, "Blessed are the barren, and the wombs that never bore, and the breasts that never nursed"' (Luke 23:28, 29). This is of a piece with Jesus' challenge to the gender and family stereotypes whereby women find their highest calling as wives and mothers, and blood-related families form the foundations of God's people (Luke 8:1-3, 19-21; 11:27). Jesus does not deny that children are a gift from God. But he enlarges the sphere of grace by suggesting that childlessness can also be a gift of God.

As with all such gifts the most appropriate question is not, 'Why has their gift been withheld from me?', but 'What am I to do with the gift that is mine?' This may not remove the pain of unwanted childlessness, but it offers a different perspective on an unwelcome condition. Like Paul's enigmatic and abiding 'thorn in the flesh' (2 Corinthians 12:7-9), childlessness may draw individuals and couples nearer to the weakness of Christ, where they will find resources to affirm their own gift and calling.

Story

A 3-year-old is talking to her mother about what she wants to be when she grows up. 'I want to be a ballerina, to make cakes, to grow flowers and be a mummy.' The first three may fade, but the fourth is likely to last, because it is an identity that is modelled from our earliest days and rehearsed through the body's own cycles. In a world with ever-widening opportunities for women, we may wonder how the mother might respond to her daughter's ambitions.

Thought to take away

There need be no shame in being childless today. But it can be devastating if it is not from choice. What do the counter-cultural values of Jesus add to the empathy and sensitivity that are the hallmarks of compassion?

---

6. According to a study carried out on 98,000 women in Denmark, published by the European Society for Human Reproduction and Embryology in 2012, cited on www.infertilitynetwork.com. Accessed 11 July 2012.

Conflict

Robert Reiss

If you are offering your gift at the altar, and there remember that your brother has something against you, leave your gift there before the altar and go; first be reconciled to your brother, and then come and offer your gift.

Matthew 5:24 (Revised Standard Version)

Background information

Conflict of some form is almost inevitable in life. The conflict might be a deep and very long-lasting one between whole communities, as, for example, between Israelis and Arabs, or between Protestants and Catholics in Northern Ireland, the latter conflict happily lessened now. At the core of such conflicts there are often arguments over scarce resources, who owns what land or who has access to what jobs. Such conflicts can be exacerbated by other more subtle conflicts, for example ones over values. They may be different values between different cultures, or ones simply between individuals, as in political debates between those who advocate freedom and those who advocate equality. Other conflicts, although at one level less serious, can be about norms of behaviour; table manners within a family for example. Conflict can take many forms.

Sermon ideas

Imagine you are in a conflict somewhere, any of the sorts of conflicts mentioned above, what would be your immediate reaction? One of the most basic decisions to be made almost immediately is between fight or flight. When some conflicts present themselves, simply getting out of the way might well be the most sensible option, flight is not always unwise. But if you decide to stand your ground and at least metaphorically to fight, how do you go about doing it? Is your response more likely to make the conflict worse until it is resolved in your favour, or do you look for another form of resolution?

Answers to those questions will inevitably depend upon the nature of the conflict, but unless the conflict is very clearly and unambiguously between good and evil, and few conflicts are quite as unambiguous as that, the first step should be a process of careful analysis. What is this conflict about, both on the surface but also under the surface? Is it one that can be resolved by the discovery of simple facts, or does it mean untangling issues such as the perception of history, of values or of norms of behaviour? Once the nature of the conflict with its various strands has been analysed, an attempt can then be made to see whether both sides agree with the analysis and can then move to find an agreed resolution. That is what Jesus appeared to be advocating in the verse from St Matthew's Gospel. But if an agreed analysis or resolution cannot be found, then what are the possibilities?

Not all conflicts have to be resolved. Agreeing to disagree is a perfectly reasonable option in some matters. But some major conflicts go too deep for that, and the worst outcome is some sort of tit-for-tat violent response, as happened in Northern Ireland and still happens in the Middle East. The evidence seems to be that such conflicts can only come to some sort of resolution if one or both sides voluntarily decide not to retaliate but simply to absorb some of the pain. Only then is there any chance of the pattern of retaliation being brought to an end and some sort of deeper resolution found.

From the Christian perspective that sort of absorbing of suffering for the sake of bringing peace and reconciliation can be seen in Jesus' response to the Cross. 'Father, forgive them, for they know not what they do.'

Story

At the height of the conflict in Northern Ireland a group from the Protestant side, including one of the Anglican bishops in the Province, sought to establish conversations with the IRA to see if there was any way of moving to a resolution. When it became known that these contacts were being made, some others on the Protestant side started a process of vilification of their co-religionists for even starting such talks. The bishop involved said on one occasion, 'Christians, of all people, should not be surprised to find that reconciliation is a costly business.'

Thought to take away

If establishing reconciliation in a conflict often requires sacrifice, what sacrifice might you be prepared to make to resolve any conflicts in which you are engaged?

Depression

Siobhán O'Keeffe

I wait for the Lord, my soul waits,
and in his word I hope;
my soul waits for the Lord
more than those who watch for the morning,
more than those who watch for the morning.

Psalm 130:5, 6

Background information

These words from Psalm 130 may be the heartfelt prayer of the person living through the pain of depression. In their anguish they cry to God to rescue them from the clouds of sadness that envelop their soul.

The word 'depression' is loosely used in society today but what is 'this thing' of which we speak? Depression is a serious illness that may affect anybody at any time in their lives. It is no respecter of age, social class or gender. The incidence tends to be higher in women than men. Children and teenagers may also be affected, either by experiencing the illness themselves or witnessing the suffering of a loved one. Depression is an illness that may be caused by many different factors and early recognition and treatment are vital if much unnecessary suffering is to be avoided. Some of the factors that may cause a depression are the following:

- A chemical imbalance in the body may leave the person vulnerable to suffering.
- A genetic predisposition may be culpable.
- Depression may occur when a person is experiencing difficult life events. This form of reactive depression may resolve when these events have been resolved or come to an end.

Principle features of depression include:

- sleep disturbance
- mood changes
- altered eating patterns where a loss of appetite or excessive eating may occur
- inappropriate use of drugs, alcohol or escapism in TV or other media
- difficulty concentrating on everyday tasks

- a loss of confidence
- social isolation, as the person does not feel able to participate in social events.

The feelings associated with a 'blue mood' or 'a bad day' are not the same as the excruciating pain of a bad depression. By its very nature, depression robs people of joy and hope. If severe depression is not treated quickly and appropriately, the person may become overwhelmed by the pain that they are feeling. They may contemplate or commit suicide.

Sermon ideas

'I have come that they may have life and have it to the full' (John 10:10, NIV) is one of the great promises of Jesus to all people. However, the vibrancy of spirit that we all desire can be greatly diminished when the black veil of depression overshadows our lives. When we feel weighed down by anxiety and the cares of the world, the rich promises of God seem far away from our troubled hearts. We need to hear the reassuring voice of another on our journey to a new and fuller life.

The quiet presence, word of encouragement or challenge that each person needs is different. The solidarity of spirit that is necessary is without question if hope is to be rekindled and joy restored.

As a Christian community we are asked to accompany each other on our pilgrimage through life. Each life has its own share of joy and sorrow but we do not travel alone. Our compassionate God journeys with us. He reaches out to us through the healing power of his word and the love and concern of each other. He reminds us: 'I have loved you with an everlasting love; therefore I have continued my faithfulness to you' (Jeremiah 31:3). He asks us to be vigilant to the needs of each other and respond in a timely and appropriate manner to the distress of each other.

Today the media bombards our senses with 'bad news'. Our hope is sapped when we read of recession, unemployment, street crime, natural disasters. It is easy to become despondent or even depressed when faced with a litany of disasters. The human spirit is resilient but we all say, 'We can only take so much suffering, grief or loss.' The person with a pre-disposition to a depressive illness may be at risk of sinking into a mire of despair when they open their morning newspaper over breakfast. The joy that filled their soul on waking to the sound of birdsong evaporates more fully with every page that they turn. Coffee grows cold and spirits sink. Clouds of sadness invade the spirit and the person may feel, 'What is the point of going to work if my job is about to be axed?' Factors outside of my control have placed a strain on my relationships and my finances are in a mess. A cry of anguish bursts forth from the soul,

> Out of the depths I cry to you, O Lord.
> Lord, hear my voice!
> Let your ears be attentive to the voice of my
> supplications! (Psalm 130:1)

At the hour of greatest need, a compassionate companion listens to the distress of the afflicted person. They hear the anguish of soul and offer a word of consolation and hope.

'My God will fully satisfy every need of yours according to his riches in glory in Christ Jesus' (Philippians 4:19). This is not offered as a platitude or in a patronising manner but tries to reassure the person that God is with them and will help them in their everyday struggle. A compassionate, listening presence may help the person to keep hope alive and their situation in perspective. The ill person may also be supported to seek appropriate medical help or counselling which will aid recovery. This is a fleshing out of the unconditional love and promises of God.

Story

A young man returned seriously injured from fighting on the front line of war. Many of his friends and colleagues had fallen before his eyes. Some left wives and children behind. All were in their 20s. They had been friends since their first day in the regiment. Michael had suffered multiple serious injuries when he had stepped on a bomb. He was told by his doctor that he would lose both legs. He would need months of rehabilitation to regain some independence. He was totally devastated by the loss of his friends and feared for his own future. His sense of loss and grief were overwhelming. He did not feel able to talk about his experience and became increasingly withdrawn and depressed. He sat alone in his room for hours. His family and friends were unable to reach him as his spirits sank lower and lower into a mire of despair. He even contemplated suicide.

He had always been a man of faith and had prayed every day of his life until that fateful day. Now God seemed absent and he felt so alone. Nothing could ease the overwhelming sense of sadness that pervaded his soul. One day the hospital chaplain visited as usual. He sat quietly with Michael and invoked the Holy Spirit to guide him in his ministry to this beloved child of God. He prayed that the darkness might give way to light and a new dawn might be born.

'Nothing can separate us from the love of God' were the words that filled the room. The young man raised his head, opened his eyes and a half-smile crossed his face for the first time in many months. He began to pour out the sadness that weighed upon him and the tears flowed like rivers. The chaplain listened and gently supported his young friend through his journey to the cross. Healing had begun.

Months of physical rehabilitation, psychological therapy and spiritual direction followed. The courage that had sustained Michael on the front line helped him slowly to rebuild his life. The love and support of a wonderful, caring family and hospital staff renewed his sense of hope. A new day was dawning.

A few years later Michael volunteered to support other returning soldiers in rebuilding their lives. He wanted to share what God in his goodness had done for him. He wanted to renew the hope of his brothers and sisters who had been willing to lay down their lives in the cause of peace. He wished to be a partaker in the 'up-building' of God's kingdom on earth. He gave thanks for the love and support of all who had stood by him in his trials and wished to give thanks in real and tangible ways.

Thought to take away

Am I available to listen and respond to the cry of the person who is struggling to keep their hope alive today? Am I willing to seek help for any depression or despondency that I may be experiencing at this time? Do I believe in God's unconditional love for me?

God reminds us all of how special we are to him. 'I have loved you with an everlasting love' (Jeremiah 31:3). We are each other's keeper and have a duty of care to walk with each other through the difficult times in life. We can all do our little bit to make the world a happier place for all. Let us commit ourselves to sharing that love and help to make life better for each other each day.

Deprivation

Paul Nicholson

While Jesus was at Bethany in the house of Simon the leper, as he sat at the table, a woman came with an alabaster jar of very costly ointment of nard, and she broke open the jar and poured the ointment on his head. But some were there who said to one another in anger, 'Why was the ointment wasted in this way? For this ointment could have been sold for more than three hundred denarii, and the money given to the poor.' And they scolded her. But Jesus said, 'Let her alone; why do you trouble her? She has performed a good service for me. For you always have the poor with you, and you can show kindness to them whenever you wish; but you will not always have me. She has done what she could; she has anointed my body beforehand for its burial. Truly I tell you, wherever the good news is proclaimed in the whole world, what she has done will be told in remembrance of her.'

Mark 14:3-9

Background information

Every three years since 2004 the United Kingdom government has produced an 'Index of Multiple Deprivation', allowing geographical areas to be ranked relative to each other according to their level of deprivation.[7] This is then used to target government responses. The 2010 report shows over 5 million people living within the most deprived areas of the UK. Attempts have been made to produce a similar measure on a worldwide basis, but are hampered by debate about what constitutes deprivation in different societies and cultures.

Sermon ideas

What mental image is conjured up when you hear the word 'deprivation'? Perhaps that of a starving child in sub-Saharan Africa, or of a Big Issue seller on a city street. Yet a moment's reflection will suggest many other aspects of deprivation. Those who leave school with inadequate qualifications, or face the break-up of marriage and family, or find themselves lonely and isolated in old age – each, however wealthy, is undoubtedly deprived. Often, too, different kinds of deprivation can go together. An old person living in sub-standard accommodation on a small pension, uncared for because family and friends are either dead or far away, suffers from multiple deprivation. How should a Christian respond to these situations?

The first impulse may well be to want to *do* something, take some immediate action. Those around Jesus in Mark's Gospel seem genuine in their desire to sell this precious ointment to raise money for the relief of poverty. Jesus doesn't discount this kind of response; indeed, he points out that occasions for it will never be lacking. But he also invites them to look more deeply.

He himself is about to be arrested on trumped-up charges, condemned in a show-trial, and executed in a barbarous fashion. All this, surely, constitutes deprivation, of liberty and of life itself. It is not a matter of trying to weigh the relative merits of this against the needs of those who might have been helped by the ointment's sale. Rather, the woman who ministers to Jesus has done what she was able to, and done it out of love. As a guide to a Christian response to deprivation, this will take us a long way.

The so-called 'pastoral cycle' suggests that any response starts with an experience of deprivation, my own or that of others. This leads to analysis and reflection: why are these people deprived, and how might the situation be improved? Next comes action, the attempt to do something to ameliorate some aspect of the encountered deprivation. This leads into further experience, and so the cycle starts again. Some will be gifted in standing alongside the deprived, sharing and perhaps articulating their experience, while others will be skilled in analysis, and others again in taking direct action of one kind or another. There is no single Christian response to deprivation. Rather, as Paul's image of the body and its members suggest, only together can we adequately meet the needs of those around us.

Story

Dom Helder Camara was Roman Catholic Archbishop of Recife, an impoverished area of north-east Brazil, between 1964 and 1985. One of the great practical exponents of liberation theology, he said: 'When I feed the poor they call me a saint. When I ask why so many people are poor they call me a communist.' In his view, Christians were to be committed not simply to charitable work to mitigate the effects of deprivation, but also to the complex social and political analysis that would uncover its roots and causes.

Thought to take away

What is the connection between poverty and deprivation? Some religious people freely choose to live lives of poverty without, presumably, feeling that they are deprived in doing so. But is involuntary poverty necessarily a factor in deprivation? Does the idea of deprivation imply that someone is to blame, by depriving me of something that is my due? Many of the deprived are also poor, and vice-versa. Yet it seems clear that the two concepts are not exactly the same. In what areas of life do you consider yourself to be deprived?

7. The most recent figures, for 2010, can be found here: www.communities.gov.uk/publications/corporate/statistics/indices2010.

Despair

Helen Costigane

O that my vexation were weighed,
and all my calamity laid in the balances!
For then it would be heavier than the sand of the sea;
therefore my words have been rash.

Job 6:2, 3

Background information

There is no one single cause of despair. It may arise from serious medical problems, physical and mental, or from abusive relationships that destroy our confidence and self-esteem. Other factors that might lead to it include overwork, stress, financial problems and substance misuse which may make us more vulnerable to feelings of hopelessness and defeat. Despair may be temporary, brought about by extreme circumstances, or it may be a long-term and unwelcome tormentor.

Sermon ideas

Just like others, those who believe in God are not immune from such feelings of emptiness or despair, which can arise from external factors such as redundancy, breakdowns in key relationships, or a total reversal of fortunes. The story of Job, a rich and happy man who was a faithful servant of God, is a case in point. He is tested by God, losing children, possessions and his health, and the words above reflect the depth of his misery which is impossible to measure. At the same time, Job refuses to lose faith in God.

Despair may also come in the form of feelings of hopelessness in our expectation of God's mercy and forgiveness. The story of the death of Judas in Matthew's Gospel more than suggests that though Judas exhibited remorse for betraying Jesus, he despaired of being forgiven (Matthew 27:3-5). This contrasts with Peter's repentance while, knowing only too well his own betrayal of Jesus, he somehow carried on in the hope that the Jesus he knew would bring him forgiveness and healing.

The antidote to despair in the words of St Francis of Assisi is 'hope'. Human hope, the product of our efforts, can make life on earth bearable. Yet, this is not enough. What is needed is divine hope, the understanding that God is active in our lives. God holds out hope to us so that our lives are anchored in him (Hebrews 6:19, 20) so that, joyful in hope, we may persevere (Romans 12:12) and become the people that God calls us to be.

Story

Once upon a time I was falling in love,
but now I'm only falling apart.
There's nothing I can do –
a total eclipse of the heart.[8]

The words in this song, originally sung by Bonnie Tyler, capture well some of the underlying aspects of 'despair' – a total loss or absence of hope, a feeling of being overcome by a sense of futility or defeat, and total darkness in terms of emotions. This is illustrated in the film, *An Officer and a Gentleman*, in which we learn about Sid who joined the US Navy's Aviator Officer Candidate School. Having suffered an anxiety attack, he comes to realise that he only entered the programme out of a sense of obligation to his family, and so he drops out. He proposes to his girlfriend, Lynette, believing her to be pregnant, and she tells him that she had lied about this to get him to propose. Not only this, but Lynette rejects Sid – she only wants to marry a naval aviator, not someone who lives in a one-horse town, as he does. Feeling scorned, humiliated and hopeless, he checks into a motel and commits suicide.

Thought to take away

Challenges for us include developing a healthy sense of self and learning to love ourselves as well as our neighbour (Mark 12:31), and reminding ourselves that we are not defined by what we possess (Psalm 49:16-18). Further, we need to remember that God invites us always to seek comfort and healing from him (Matthew 11:28) – and to continue to hope in him and his promises to us.

8. 'Total eclipse of the heart', © Copyright Jim Steinman (Columbia Music Group, 1983).

Discipline

Tony Castle

Do you not know that in a race all the runners run, but only one gets the prize? Run in such a way as to get the prize. Everyone who competes in the games goes into strict training. They do it to get a crown that will not last; but we do it to get a crown that will last for ever.

1 Corinthians 9:24, 25 (New International Version)

Background information

The Olympic Games are long expected, then they are taking place and suddenly they are over and history! Wherever they are staged they are accompanied by much hype. Sights are already set on the 2016 Games in Rio de Janeiro, Brazil. But behind the scenes in swimming pools, on running and cycling tracks around the world the athletes will be keeping up the training. They have to remain disciplined. If, for example, you are a swimmer, you will need to be up at 4.30am every day, in the pool by 5am then pounding up and down the pool for three hours before going to school or work. Such discipline! Without that strict discipline there can be no success. An English swimmer pinned up on her locker door a small poster that read, 'No pain, no gain: no guts no glory.'

The word *discipline* comes from the Latin and originates from the word *discipulus* (disciple). St Paul would have been very aware of this and he draws the two concepts together in his letter to the Christians of Corinth. Referring to the famous Isthmian Games held near Corinth, he says that competitors go into strict training to win a crown that will not last, but we, disciples of Christ, are disciplined in order to 'get a crown that will last for ever'.

Sermon ideas

When we speak of discipline the words 'spare the rod and spoil the child' come to mind. This admonition has had a long history in English literature from the poem *Piers Plowman* written by Langland in 1377 to Samuel Butler's *Hudibras* of 1662. The original source is the first part of Proverbs 13:24. The second part reads 'he who loves his son is careful to discipline him' (NIV). We should carefully note that Scripture places the disciplining of a child in the context of love. If we change the two words 'the rod', which jar on our modern ears, to 'correction', we get, 'if you do not correct your child you will spoil him or her'.

So in a home or school setting, what is 'the correction' and discipline for? And, how should it be administered? We need to explore the connection between 'discipline' and 'disciple'. A disciple is someone who follows a teacher in order to learn. In our case we follow Jesus in order to learn and live by his Good News. Our teacher commands us to love God with the whole of our being and 'love your neighbour as yourself' (Luke 10:27). That requires a lot of self-discipline and self-control that is not natural to us. Our instincts for self-preservation and self-interest are natural to the human person; self-denial and self-control are not. So we are good, faithful disciples to the degree that we are self-disciplined. St Paul is quite explicit that if we do not discipline ourselves we will not 'get a crown that will last for ever'.

The aim, then, of external, imposed discipline on a child or young person, by parent or teacher, is to help that person to come gradually to an interior self-discipline. *The Times* newspaper (13 August 2011) carried an article on family discipline; it gave this parental advice, 'Correct firmly. Say, No, we are not doing that.' Be warm but be firm. From the Christian perspective, keeping in mind the Lord's teaching on love, all correction, whether in the home or the school, should be firm but warm.

Story

Martine Wright's day, on the morning of 7 July 2005, got off to a sluggish start. She had spent the night before celebrating London winning the 2012 Olympic Games vote with 'a couple of beers', with work colleagues. Hurrying for work she discovered that she had to use the Circle Line. She found a seat, but didn't notice the man with a rucksack who got on and stood close to her. After the explosion she was in such a total physical mess that she remained an unidentified victim of the London bombings for 36 hours. They had to take away both legs, almost to the waist! Then, within days, Martine started the fight back. With great mental discipline she co-operated with the medical teams. Then, once she had learnt to get around on her stumps, she heard of the British Paralympic Association and the new sport of sitting volleyball.

Acceptance on the Olympic team became her target. With a very disciplined lifestyle and hard work she made it to represent her country.

Thought to take away

We need to be convinced of the need for discipline, whether this is in the home, school or in our own private lives. The writer to the Hebrews (12:11) says 'no discipline seems pleasant . . . Later on, however, it produces a harvest of righteousness and peace' (NIV). It should always be administered with Christ's commandment of love in mind; so we should always 'be warm but be firm'.

Discrimination

Paul Nicholson

The next day Jesus decided to go to Galilee. He found Philip and said to him, 'Follow me.' Now Philip was from Bethsaida, the city of Andrew and Peter. Philip found Nathanael and said to him, 'We have found him about whom Moses in the law and also the prophets wrote, Jesus son of Joseph from Nazareth.' Nathanael said to him, 'Can anything good come out of Nazareth?' Philip said to him, 'Come and see.'

John 1:43-46

Background information

In dealing with discrimination, the government of the United Kingdom defines nine 'protected characteristics'. People are protected by law from being discriminated against on the basis of any one of these. The nine are:

- race
- sex
- sexual orientation
- disability (or because of something connected with a disability)
- religion or belief
- being a transsexual person
- having just had a baby or being pregnant
- being married or in a civil partnership (this applies only at work or if someone is being trained for work)
- age (this applies only at work or if someone is being trained for work)

The point of the protection is that these are the characteristics that are most likely to be the subject of prejudice, judgements made in advance about people that have little to do with their actual characters or abilities. The same source recognises that there are, however, situations in which it may be lawful to restrict the provision of goods and services to one section of a population.

Sermon ideas

'Can anything good come out of Nazareth?', Nathanael asks. We know that at this point he hasn't met Jesus; his remark is simply based on prejudice. It is worth noticing Philip's response. In this instance, he doesn't condemn Nathanael, or even argue with him. He simply invites him to come and experience this new preacher, with as open a heart and mind as he can muster. And it works. In the following verses, Nathanael has been won over by Jesus to the extent that he makes more extravagant claims about who this man is than even Philip has done.

It is all too easy to dismiss individuals, groups, or even whole populations on the basis of hearsay, or by lazily going along with popular opinion. It is clearly not humanly possible to experience everything, so a certain prejudging is one way of enabling us to cope with a diverse and complex world. This is necessary, but becomes harmful when it cuts us off from new experience, determining who we will and will not meet, where we will and will not go. Nor is prejudice something that simply harms the one who is thus prejudiced. In those situations where I have power, or am in control – for instance, enjoying the role of determining who will have access to goods, benefits, or even other people – prejudice on my part can have a hugely detrimental effect on others.

Often legal intervention is seen as the best way of dealing with prejudice. In recent decades many governments have enacted wide-ranging legislation to try to combat discrimination based on prejudice. There is clearly a challenge in determining when there are legitimate grounds for discrimination – few would deny that convicted paedophiles should have their subsequent access to children restricted, but few cases are so clear. Christians will sometimes find themselves accused of prejudice when in their own eyes they are simply upholding their own values in such areas as marriage and community leadership.

The example of Nathanael perhaps points to a strategy that can sometimes address issues of prejudice at a level deeper than legislation can touch. If those thought to be prejudiced can be persuaded to experience the situation or group whom they are reacting against, they may find their prejudices challenged or even overthrown. Such a situation is often not easy to engineer, and a key prerequisite is that the prejudiced party should be helped to feel safe in the encounter. Yet this is surely a valuable undertaking for those who follow the one who declared that peacemakers are blessed.

Story

Perhaps the greatest ever example of rhetoric directed against prejudice was the speech given by Martin Luther King Jr on 28 August 1963 from the steps of the Lincoln Memorial in Washington DC. Initially heard by more than 200,000 participants in the March for Jobs and Freedom, the speech, with its repeated line 'I have a dream', is now known around the world. It is a powerful call for prejudice to be resisted and overcome, not through violence, but by 'meeting physical force with soul force'. Luther King's words demonstrate the power of inspiration in overcoming social ills. They also show the price that must often be paid for such a stance. Five years after making this speech, he was assassinated for his work in opposing racial discrimination.

Thought to take away

Prejudice is always easier to recognise in others than in myself. Indeed, my own prejudices are almost by definition something that I am, at least initially, unaware of. Yet no one is without prejudice. Christian growth involves slowly coming to awareness of those areas in which I am likely to discriminate unjustly, and to allow my attitudes and responses here to be challenged. If the limits of my own experience are often at the root of my prejudices, the answer may well be to take opportunities to step beyond what is most familiar to me, and take positive steps to meet new people, visit strange places, and engage with unfamiliar situations.

Embryology

Brian Fahy

People even brought little children to him, for him to touch them; but when the disciples saw this they turned them away. But Jesus called the children to him and said, 'Let the little children come to me, and do not stop them; for it is to such as these that the kingdom of God belongs. I tell you solemnly, anyone who does not welcome the kingdom of God like a little child will never enter it.'

Luke 18:15-17 (Jerusalem Bible)

Background information

Over recent decades, medical science has made rapid progress and has developed many technologies to address issues surrounding human fertility. Studies of human life in its basic structures and of the human embryo, have enabled scientists to propose and to develop various techniques aimed at helping infertile couples to have children. These new developments have opened up many possibilities, which demand ethical and legal review. In vitro fertilisation and embryo transfer, artificial insemination by husband, or by donor, surrogate motherhood and 'saviour siblings' are some of the recent developments that call for our attention and evaluation.

In the United Kingdom, the Warnock Report (1984) preceded legislation in the form of the Human Embryology and Fertilisation Bill. This study gave a positive endorsement, with legal and social cautions, to medical advances surrounding fertility, and to embryo research, but also included dissent from those conclusions by some members of the committee.

The Church of England also produced a report on the subject, 'Embryo Research: Some Christian Perspectives' in 2008. This report gave a cautious affirmation to embryo research, on the grounds of the undefined status of the embryo in its first days, and in consideration of the benefits that could accrue.

The Catholic Church published its teaching in the document, Donum Vitae (1987) and the encyclical, Evangelium Vitae (1995). Catholic teaching takes a definite position on the status of the human embryo from its first moment, according it the value of a human person. Therapeutic intervention for the well-being of the embryo is recognised, but no form of research or experimentation is acceptable.

Sermon ideas

Respect for human life is often in short supply. The shock of the First World War, and the millions of lives lost in the trenches and on the battlefields of Flanders, demonstrated a callous disregard for the value of the human person. This, in turn, caused people to lose respect for the authority of State and Church, which had encouraged such frightening slaughter. How could leaders send so many people to their deaths so easily and so heartlessly. The voice of the people, the many and varied voices, has grown ever since, and the ways of democracy demand a public consensus to emerge when laws and policy are made. This consensus, and the debate which must precede it, is especially important where matters of life and death are involved.

With the onward march of science during this time, the voice of religion has been diminished. Belief in God has been awarded a quiet place in private human conscience, and provided that it does not harm others, religion is allowed its place, its much-reduced place in civic society. Religious belief is regarded by many as a relic of a past age and as an anomaly in this age of scientific rationalism. Yet it would be a great mistake for either side to be dismissive of the other. As Pope John Paul II said, in his address to the United Nations in 1995, we 'must find a way to discuss the human future intelligibly'.

The starting point for such a discussion is to be found in the value of the human person. Religious teaching promotes this value, which finds its echo in society's emphasis on the rights of the individual. The United Nations Charter of 1945 was a reaction and a response to the deaths of millions in the great wars. No longer would human rights be trodden down. Today we promote the human individual as the greatest thing to be protected. The individual and the rights of the individual. The danger with this starting point is 'individualism', which is a concept of human isolation, whereas the 'human person' has both individual and social dimensions. The rights of the individual have led to the desire for individual choice to be perceived as a supreme value in human, moral behaviour. This has seen the practice of abortion and a woman's right to choose becoming enshrined in law.

It was concern for the rights of women, and for the health of women, and for the freedom from oppression of women, that the Abortion Law was introduced. The motivation was good, but the solution is misguided, not to say tragic. For it involves the death of the foetus in the womb, of the unborn child. A child's life does not begin at the moment of being born. There are nine months of gestation before that great moment, and the moment of conception is widely accepted by priest and scientist, as the decisive moment when new life begins.

In the field of embryology, it is the precise value to be placed on that new life that is at issue. Is this 'human material' that can helpfully be used for gaining valuable medical knowledge? The Anglican Church is sympathetic to this view. Or, is this a new human being in its very earliest form, as the Catholic Church says? Again, it is concern for people who suffer infertility, and concern for people with incurable diseases, that prompts us to do research on human embryos. Again, the motivation is good, but, in the Catholic view, the pathway is misguided, for it is not right to 'use' another human being in any way.

Is it the fact that the embryo is so small, so unseen, that causes us to think and act in this way? There is a story in the gospel of how people were bringing little children to Jesus for him to touch them, and the disciples turned them away. Little children are not so important, it would seem. But Jesus stopped them. 'Let the children come to me,' he said. We are of equal value and importance at every stage of our life.

There is no 'moral high ground' here that people need to claim. The Church, Catholic and Protestant, cares about children. The secular humanist cares about children and about fertility issues. Our differences concern our understanding of what it is to be human. We need to learn how to speak with one another about these things, and to avoid demonising one another, in the process.

There are areas of considerable disagreement here. The beginning of life and medical research, the end of life and euthanasia. The great challenge to the Church and to all Christian people is to engage with these controversial subjects in the same way that Jesus did with his opponents. Never, in any of his encounters, does the Lord insult or verbally abuse others. He speaks respectfully to everyone, even to the soldier who struck him across the face. We must learn to respect our opponents, and all those whose views differ from our own.

Story

A man was sitting at his breakfast one morning, reading the paper, when he came across an article about the latest developments in medical science. 'Donating eggs and sperm for human fertilisation banks should become as common as giving blood,' was the story. The man shook his head. What is the world coming to, he thought.

The man's son was in the next room, a student of law, home from university. The man decided to share this story with his son. What would the younger man make of it? The son listened to his father as he read out the article, and thought quietly for a while. Then he replied to his father, 'They won't stop, you know. They won't go back.'

It made the older man think. Here he was thinking in morality terms, and here was his son, thinking in reality terms. 'I guess that sums up the way we are these days. The world is always moving forward, learning and doing new things. But is it always progress? Not every road is a highway. Some are dead ends.' It made him think of the road to Emmaus, and the two disciples walking down it.

Christian and secular humanist walk the same road of life together. We must keep on talking to one another, and look to the Lord to walk with us.

Thought to take away

The psalmist of old asked the question, 'What is man that you are mindful of him and the son of man that you care for him?' (Psalm 8:4). People today ask the same question. If there is no God and no heavenly destination, then we are free to do the best we can, according to our lights. But how bright are our lights? Do we truly understand our own nature?

Euthanasia

Brendan Geary

You must not kill.

Deuteronomy 5:17 (New Jerusalem Bible)

Be compassionate just as your Father is compassionate.

Luke 6:36 (New Jerusalem Bible)

Background information

Recent polls have shown that there are large majorities in favour of allowing doctors to facilitate the ending of a patient's life. If you listen to discussion programmes, radio phone-ins or programmes like Question Time on BBC 1, this topic continually generates strong feelings on both sides. Those who are in favour of what is called 'Assisted dying' refer to freedom of choice and the alleviation of unnecessary suffering. Those who are opposed often cite the biblical injunction that we should not kill, refer to the dangers inherent in legal provisions to end a person's life, and the advances in palliative care, especially in hospices, when caring for those who are dying. Both sides use the importance of human dignity in death as part of their argument. Laws supporting assisted dying have already been introduced in Belgium, The Netherlands and Luxembourg, and in the American states of Oregon, Washington and Montana.

Sermon ideas

Advances in medicine have enabled us to continue life beyond what was possible not too long ago. Some people ask if modern medicine is always our ally, or if it can sometimes interfere with the natural processes leading to death. St Francis referred to 'Sister Death,' acknowledging that death is part of life. None of us wishes to see the death of a loved one, with the loss and sense of emptiness that this brings. At the same time, we do not want to watch those whom we care for suffer, especially if they have been diagnosed with a terminal, incurable illness.

This topic elicits strong emotions on both sides. Many people, particularly those who come from a religious background, have deep convictions about the sanctity of life, and the dangers of providing legal protection for those who are prepared to assist those who wish to die. In The Netherlands not long ago a Catholic priest refused to allow a funeral liturgy in the parish church for a man who had died through voluntary euthanasia. Support for the Dutch hierarchy's position regarding euthanasia in this case was clear, but many felt there was a lack of compassion in this response.[9] Some Christians refer to 'a consistent ethic of life,'[10] that seeks to protect life from conception to natural death, and this includes respect for the sincerely held views of others.

There are others, including Christians, who consider that the human impulse to be compassionate is applicable in some cases. The Falconer Commission in the United Kingdom (2012), for example, argued in favour of assisted dying if the following conditions are met:

- the person is over 18 years of age
- the person is terminally ill (defined as having fewer than 12 months to live)
- the person is not mentally impaired
- the person is acting according to their wishes alone, and is not being unduly influenced by others, especially those who may benefit materially from their death.

Those who oppose assisted dying will argue that it is impossible to predict accurately how long a person will live, that people's mental states can change quickly, and that it is difficult to be sure that someone's decision is not influenced by the wishes of others. The poet Arthur Hugh Clough famously wrote:

> Thou shalt not kill: but needst not strive
> officiously to keep alive.[11]

There is a certain wisdom in this tradition. It is possible to oppose an intervention to bring death about, while at the same time declining extraordinary means to keep the person alive.

Story

Pope John Paul II gave a powerful example of this towards the end of his life. He could have stayed in hospital being cared for, thereby extending his life. He chose, however, to return to the Vatican – to return home – and allow life to take its natural course. The last days of Blessed John Paul II were marked by dignity and serenity, and his death left its mark on the world.

Thought to take away

Jesus spent a significant part of his ministry alleviating suffering and curing various illnesses. At the same time, his death and resurrection challenge a culture that fears death and sees no meaning in suffering. We must have compassion and show understanding for those who act to end the suffering of others through assisted dying, while upholding the value of life and respecting the natural processes of life – which include death. A Christian response involves making the political choices to ensure that we provide the resources necessary for a dignified end to a person's life.

9. Dutch euthanasia case gives double verdict, *The Tablet*, 10 September 2011, p.29.
10. Joseph Bernardin, *A Consistent Ethic of Life: An American-Catholic Dialogue*, Gannon Lecture, Fordham University, 6 December 1983. http://www.priestsforlife.org/magisterium/bernardingannon.html (retrieved 13 June 2012).
11. *The Latest Decalogue* from *The Poems of Arthur Clough*, ed. A. L. P. Norrington, 1968.

Exorcism

Edgar Ruddock

Then Jesus summoned his twelve disciples and gave them authority over unclean spirits, to cast them out, and to cure every disease and every sickness.

Matthew 10:1

(For examples of exorcism see Mark 4:35–5:20; Luke 11:14-20.)

Background information

Throughout history, Christians – and the churches they belong to – have had to find ways of understanding, confronting and overcoming evil. Exorcism has been the Church's way of dealing with individual manifestations of 'possession' by 'evil spirits'. In some circumstances this has proved to be a powerful gospel weapon, leading to healing, reconciliation and hope. More often, sadly, it has become an abusive tool to exercise power and control of a different sort, and has led to psychological trauma, and an increase in both alienation and fear.

Most churches have a designated officer for dealing with issues of spiritual powers/possession/exorcism.

Historically the issue has often involved dealing with the unknown. As science has advanced, there is more and more explanation, so there is less of the unknown to confound us.

Sermon ideas

When Jesus cast out demons, he was dealing with a wide range of issues that today we might handle differently. 'Possession' was a commonly understood way of describing how people were taken over by things over which they had no control. What might those parallels be today?

- How do we deal with fear?
- How do we handle the unknown?
- What is our experience of addiction?
- How do we deal with obsessions about prosperity, sex, or self-image?

Our modern society is so good at hurling images, advertising, music and peer-group pressures at us, that we seldom have a chance to really explore our true selves. Of course much in art, music and contemporary culture is brilliant and reflects the creativity of God revealed in all God's creation, but where these are manipulated by powerful people, companies or institutions they can become both destructive and sinister. We are in a sense in danger of being 'possessed' and we do well to ask how we can find liberation from these subtle manifestations of twenty-first-century diseases.

Behind all this lies the deeper question – How do we recognise and confront the reality of evil?

There is a temptation among some Christians to resort to exorcism as a means of driving out, or destroying, what the Bible refers to as demons or evil spirits. It is interesting to note that in the story of Noah (Genesis chapters 6–8) God sees such evil in the world that he wants to start all over again, apart from Noah and his family who had found divine favour. Only later does God swear that 'never again' will he choose destruction to deal with the human condition. Rather God chooses redemption. So exorcism needs to be thought through very carefully and must be seen as an agent of redemption, not destruction.

But before we get to any stage of formal rites of the Church, we have a responsibility to use all the gifts God has already given us: the wisdom of reflection, prayer, learning, the experience of others, the skills of doctors, nurses or therapists. Jesus says 'If you have ears then hear!' – and perhaps we need to learn to listen to the wisdom of modern science, medicine, and psychology before jumping to more overtly 'spiritual' conclusions.

The number of occasions when all these resources still fail to address a real and deep need will be relatively few. The wisdom of the Church down the centuries has recognised this and provided resources of prayer and a ministry of deliverance, that will be used only by those specially trained and authorised by the Church – and after a long process of discernment.

Story

A woman brings her daughter to the priest, claiming the daughter is so wicked that she must be possessed, and asks for an exorcism to 'sort out' the recalcitrant teenager. The wise priest, of course, spends plenty of time listening to both mother and daughter. What transpires is that the daughter is rebelling against a mother who is herself terrified that the girl will make the same 'dreadful mistakes' that she did as a teenager. She has become overprotective, domineering and hypercritical. The girl, in her adolescent turbulence, doubts her mother's love for her, and so goes out to find it (and her own sense of worth) elsewhere. As both are helped to see and understand what is going on, there is a process of recognition, learning, liberation and reconnecting – a deliverance in the true sense of the word for both mother and daughter.

Thought to take away

Knowing we are loved by God, and by others, restores our identity: as we claim who we know we are, we are slowly able to find release from all that hinders our flourishing as those made in God's image, and restored to his likeness. As 'perfect love casts out fear' so we find both our deliverance and our healing, and are set free to become gift and blessing to others.

Fertility and infertility

Clare Richards

Then God remembered Rachel, and God hearkened to her and opened her womb. She conceived and bore a son, and said, 'God has taken away my reproach'; and she called his name Joseph.

Genesis 30:22-24 (Revised Standard Version)

Background information

Statistics show that an increasing number of women are finding it difficult to conceive. There is evidence that lifestyles today are contributing to fertility problems. This causes great sadness in many people's lives. Human fertility depends on a number of factors: sexual behaviour, nutrition, timing, emotions, and medical problems. Many Christians believe that as life comes from God, any help that creates new life is good. Health services in the 'developed world' give hope to those in distress. But there are no easy answers to infertility, especially as medical help is costly and time-consuming. With the exception of the Catholic and Orthodox Churches, other Churches accept medical intervention of in vitro fertilisation and artificial insemination, with some reservations. All Churches disapprove of surrogacy and the creation of 'spare' embryos for research. The Catholic Church takes the extreme hard line, not accepting any of the medical procedures.

Sermon ideas

There are a number of stories of initially infertile women in the Bible, including Sarah, Rachel, Hannah and Elizabeth.[12] The Jews saw children as a sign of God's blessing, so infertility was dreaded. Rachel, a wife of Jacob, was unable to conceive for years. When she finally gave birth to Joseph she said, 'God has taken away my reproach.' Rachel's story mirrors the feeling of desolation and failure experienced by some women who long for motherhood.

In these biblical stories God intervenes and against all probability, the women conceive. Christians believe that life is a gift from God, not a right. Many accept that medical intervention could be seen as today's intervention of God. There is disagreement among the Churches about how far this should go, but all agree that the creation of 'spare' embryos is wrong, and that surrogacy is not accepted. The Catholic Church has always taken the hard line, with strict guidelines set out in 1987, stating that the only moral route to conception is through sexual intercourse. It is clear that many Catholics make up their own minds.

There are serious moral issues that face us today, and should not be dismissed. Easy access to contraception is a concern, as it is readily available and even offered to school-age children. We should ask if contraception is now essential given the effects of fertility on the world population. How are those countries ravaged by HIV/Aids to cope without distribution of condoms? Shouldn't we be concerned for those suffering in this way? Most of us in the developed world are able to celebrate life in our families, including occasions like Mother's and Father's Day. In some of our churches we will celebrate Mothering Sunday, thought to originate from a sixteenth-century Christian custom of families meeting at the mother church to celebrate 'joyful Sunday'. The tradition is remembered by reflecting on the role of Mary, as the mother of Jesus or on the church as 'mother church'. Many parishes celebrate with children giving flowers to their mothers during the church service.

Sarah, Rachel, Hannah and Elizabeth saw their sons as 'godsends'. Christian mothers and fathers will see their children as the greatest gift God could have given them. It is Luke who is anxious to point out that it is Jesus who is the ultimate 'Godsend'. His nativity narrative sends us back to Hannah's story, a moving description of her distress at her failure to conceive a child, and her joy when God intervenes to give her a son, Samuel. It concludes with Hannah's 'magnificat', which is clearly adopted by Luke, who puts her words into Mary's mouth as she greets her cousin Elizabeth.

> 'My soul magnifies the Lord,
> and my spirit rejoices in God my Saviour,
> for he has regarded the low estate of his
> handmaiden.'
>
> *Luke 1:46-48 (Revised Standard Version)*

Luke's compassionate character shines through this Gospel, where he shows more interest in people than in ideas, having great sympathy for those in distress.

He invites us to see Christ as the great comforter, inviting us to follow his example by responding with sensitivity to those who suffer. Those who remain infertile, or have repeated miscarriages, suffer a loss for the children they never had. Many people in the world suffer the loss of their children who never survived poverty and sickness. Adoption is for some a wonderful gift from God, turning the loss into fulfilment and joy.

Story

When family or friends suffer such loss it can be difficult to know what to say.

A small child returning from a neighbour's house where her little friend had died, was asked by her father where she had been. 'To comfort her mother,' the little girl replied. Her father asked her what she had done to comfort her. 'I climbed into her lap and cried with her,' she answered.

Sometimes we can learn such sensitivity from children.

Thought to take away

The words of Mary and Hannah speak of poverty. The Magnificat has been noted as revolutionary, calling on us to reach out to those in greatest need. It reminds us in the rich world that there are those in other countries who suffer most and that we will find Christ there. 'I say to you, as you did it to the least of my brethren, you did it to me' (Matthew 25:40, RSV). Perhaps we could think of those in other parts of the world who can never get help for their infertility, and for those who have to watch their children die. What can we do about it? Christian Aid, Cafod or Tear Fund will be able to tell us, and invite us to give them support.

12. Sarah: Genesis 16–21; Rachel: Genesis 29–30; Hannah: 1 Samuel 1–2:11; Elizabeth: Luke 1:5-58.

Fortune-telling

Paul Nicholson

One day, as we were going to the place of prayer, we met a slave-girl who had a spirit of divination and brought her owners a great deal of money by fortune-telling. While she followed Paul and us, she would cry out, 'These men are slaves of the Most High God, who proclaim to you a way of salvation.' She kept doing this for many days. But Paul, very much annoyed, turned and said to the spirit, 'I order you in the name of Jesus Christ to come out of her.' And it came out that very hour. But when her owners saw that their hope of making money was gone, they seized Paul and Silas and dragged them into the market-place before the authorities.

Acts 16:16-19

Background information

There is no clear distinction to be made between divination and fortune-telling, the two characteristics (in the NRSV translation) of the slave-girl who so annoys Paul at Philippi. Both are attempts to foretell future events (or sometimes gain deeper insight into current events) by supernatural or occult means. These practices have a long history, being a feature of most recorded cultures. Specialists catalogue a range of ways in which they can be carried out: reliance on omens, the casting of lots, random consultation of a sacred text, study of the flight pattern of birds, or of the internal organs of sacrificed animals – all have been employed at one time or another. The fortune-telling can be heavily ritualised, or more spontaneous. In the United Kingdom there has long been some legal regulation of these practices, including the 1951 Fraudulent Mediums Act (recently replaced by a series of European Union Consumer Protection Regulations).

Sermon ideas

No fairground is complete without a fortune-teller's tent, complete with woman draped in shawls promising to tell your fortune with the help of her crystal ball if you cross her palm with silver. You will find the same at many a church fête. Most people probably give it little thought. If challenged, they might suggest that it is 'only a bit of a laugh'. Yet there is a strong strand of unease about the practice within Christianity which it inherited from Judaism, and which shouldn't be dismissed as mere fundamentalism even today.

One source of the unease centres around the question of the sources of the purported knowledge. In the Old Testament, King Saul consults a medium, who summons up the spirit of the dead prophet Samuel. Such disturbance of the dead is clearly against God's law. The Philippian slave-girl gains her power as a result of being possessed by a spirit; once Paul casts it out, she can no longer tell fortunes. In both cases there is a suggestion that the desire to know the future in this way exposes the questioner to occult forces that may not easily be controlled, and are best avoided. Many would have similar reservations about the contemporary use of Ouija boards, for instance, even if done playfully.

Another reason that Christians might want to avoid fortune-telling is the suggestion it makes that the future is fated, or predetermined, and cannot be shaped or affected by the actions of the one seeking to know it. Orthodox belief holds that one of God's greatest gifts to us is free will, the capacity to choose and mould our futures by our own acts here and now. The practice of fortune-telling can be seen as a practical repudiation of this belief. More, it can induce a passivity in one who, having heard the future predicted, believes that no further action on their part is profitable or even possible. Christian faith demands that we take more responsibility than this.

Having said all that, the practice at the fairground end of the spectrum probably shouldn't be taken too seriously. Few getting their palms read between the helter-skelter and the coconut-shy are likely to let what they hear determine the rest of their lives. A light touch is often a proper response to a moral challenge.

Story

In T. S. Eliot's *The Waste Land*, he pokes gentle fun at a fortune-teller:

> Madame Sosostris, famous clairvoyante,
> had a bad cold, nevertheless
> is known to be the wisest woman in Europe,
> with a wicked pack of cards.

He is writing in the aftermath of the First World War, when large-scale bereavement had led to a rise in the call for the services of mediums and other occult practitioners. Eliot illustrates a Christian refusal to take the practice seriously, rather than launching a head-on attack against it.

Thought to take away

In the Hebrew scriptures, prophets too gain a deeper insight into current and future events by their contact with the supernatural. Calling the people back to following the one true God, they are at times able to discern the future outcomes of the actions of political leaders. The Old Testament records debates of how true and false prophets are to be distinguished. Can Christian faith today offer particular insights into the future on such issues as global warming, or likely developments in the place of the family in society?

Fraud

Ray Simpson

God has told you what is good: To do justice, love kindness and walk humbly with your God . . . The voice of the Lord cries 'Can I tolerate wicked scales and a bag of dishonest weights?'

Micah 6:8b, 11 (author's own paraphrase)

Background information

The global financial crisis began with a banking collapse caused by bankers who engaged in fraud, either legally or morally, on a colossal scale, because they thought they were clever enough to get away with it. It was buttressed by consumers who pretended (to themselves or their lenders) that they could repay unaffordable loans. Banks have rigged interest rates that determine global prices of many financial products. Loan providers have required customers to agree to an extra, unexplained package which later forces them into un-repayable debt. Consumers who are in debt are offered 'a quick quid' without being told how much worse off the new loan will make them.

This crisis has pushed millions in developing countries into abject poverty, and many in our rich countries have lost jobs, homes or income. Fraud is so widespread that people can no longer trust institutions whose word was once their bond, and whose purpose was once to help savers or businesses. No wonder *The Economist* headlined a report on 13 July 2012 'The Rotten Heart of Finance'. Some penalties and changes in regulation are being introduced, but governments fear to do much lest the most powerful institutions relocate their business elsewhere. Consumers, who, although they see themselves as victims, nevertheless often see what they 'can get away with' themselves.

People now question whether capitalist societies can survive unless fraud is tackled at its roots. In the eyes of the law fraud is as varied as the regulations of numerous different bodies. In the eyes of God fraud starts in the heart.

Sermon ideas

Micah was an eighth-century BC prophet who lived in the rural town of Moresheth in the hills of Judah.

Nearly everyone had to buy food or other goods, and in order to know the price, the vendor weighed them on a pair of scales. But some vendors placed a secret weight in one of the scales. They charged for the weight, not for the goods. Psalms, Proverbs and Prophets alike condemn using a smaller set of measures to weigh what is sold, and a larger measure to weigh what is purchased. Proverbs 20:10 says a just weight is God's delight. A picture of scales of justice has become a symbol of justice systems in various English-speaking countries, which were shaped by biblical principles.

In the Torah, there are more commandments concerning the kashrut (fitness) of one's money than the kashrut of food. Deuteronomy 19:14 condemns moving a landmark, thereby obtaining extra land by fraud.

These laws are developed and expanded upon in the Jewish Mishnah and the Talmud. The Talmud denounces as fraud every mode of taking advantage of another's ignorance. Every gain obtained by betting or gambling or by raising the price of essential foods through speculation is theft. Every breach of promise in commerce is a sin.

Regulation is necessary, but it cannot get to the heart of the issue. The Holiness Code that is included in the Book of Leviticus (chapters 17-27) does not begin with particular do's and don'ts, it begins with a statement about God: 'I am holy' and the consequence that flows from it as water flows from a spring: 'You be holy, too.' A study of the word 'holy' suggests that these meanings are associated with it: whole, healthy, holistic. To be a healthy and whole society, we hate, denounce and eschew fraud, because we love our holy God. That is why in the New Testament Christians are simply asked not to defraud a brother or sister in any matter (1 Thessalonians 4:6).

Story

Paul Moore achieved fame as the whistle-blower who called for 'capitalism with a conscience.' The HBOS executive with the job of risk assessment outlined to the company's board the extent to which the unwise lending policies were putting the company and the shareholders' investments at risk. Subsequent to expressing his views he was threatened, grossly defamed by an 'independent' report prepared by the firm who worked for HBOS as auditors, and then summarily sacked. On informing his wife, she responded: 'Don't worry, Paul, it's all part of God's plan.' Some time later, when the collapse of the bank was being critically examined by a UK parliamentary Treasury Select Committee Paul felt that God prompted him to 'do it now' and supply details to the committee which were explosive. Subsequently, Sir James Crosby who as head of HBOS from 2001-2006 had fired Moore, resigned as deputy chairman of the Financial Services Authority, the body tasked by the Government to oversee the operation of the financial sector.

He has since launched three initiatives: *Banking on Change* aims to create a groundswell for honest and regulated banking; *A New Wilberforce* aims to recruit and deploy a core team of modern Wilberforces who will campaign to free the world of slavery to money; *Build a Better World* aims to develop collaborative community capitalism through thousands of social enterprises, and to change public habits through films and other media. Paul keeps a daily rhythm of prayer, and sometimes joins the monks at Ampleforth Abbey.

Thought to take away

A widely quoted tradition in the Talmud (Shabbat 31a) is that at a person's judgement in the next world, the first question that will be asked is, 'Were you honest in business?' However little or large our daily business may be, what will our answer be?

Gay marriage

Robert Reiss

You shall love your neighbour as yourself.

Mark 12:31

Background information

Attitudes towards homosexuality have changed dramatically over the last fifty years. The decriminalising of homosexual behaviour in 1967 reflected a growing unease among many at the treatment of homosexuals and since then, according to social surveys in England, there has been further change. In 1983 two out of every three of the general population thought that homosexual acts were always or mostly wrong, but by 2010 that had halved to one in three. Surveys of Christians over that same period showed a similar trend, with Anglicans almost exactly following the general population and Roman Catholics and other Christians groups only slightly more opposed. It seems today the majority of Christians in Britain do not think homosexual acts are always or mostly wrong.

If a same-sex couple chose to live together, including sharing the ownership of property, the law created difficulties for them in terms of inheritance when one died. For those and similar legal reasons, as well as for the desire to encourage where possible stable and permanent relationships, the Government of the day decided to introduce 'civil partnerships' in 2004, and since then many have welcomed the development, including many Christians. Some bishops spoke in favour of the legislation creating such partnerships in the House of Lords.

The blessing of such partnerships in public ceremonies in churches has proved more complex. Neither the Church of England nor the Roman Catholic bishops have authorised such public blessings, although in the case of the Church of England some bishops 'turn a blind eye' to such events in churches in their dioceses. When in 2012 the Government carried out a consultation exercise on whether it should take a further step and create the possibility of 'gay marriage', religious opinion was clearly divided. Some, such as liberal and reformed

Judaism and the Quaker movement welcomed the possibility, but the official response of the Church of England was strongly opposed. It argued that the view of marriage held by the State was the long-standing Christian one that it was a union between a man and a woman, that one of the purposes of marriage was the procreation of children and that any tampering with the law on marriage could lead to the disestablishment of the Church of England. They also raised the spectre that the European Court of Human Rights might force clergy to take same-sex marriages in church.

Sermon ideas

Christian opinion is divided, and there are a number of questions that need to be considered.

First, in an obviously varied general population with a number of faiths and many of no faith at all, is it possible for one body, even an established Church, to insist that its view of marriage must be the one held by all in the community?

Secondly, while the Church states that one of the purposes of marriage is procreation, that does not stop it taking the marriage of a couple well beyond childbearing age. If the church can do that for elderly people, knowing that they will not be able to meet one of the purposes of marriage, why should it not be able to do the same for a same-sex couple who wish to assert publicly their desire to fulfil one of the other purposes of marriage to live together 'for the mutual society, help and comfort that the one ought to have of the other, both in prosperity and adversity'?

Thirdly, while many doubt the probability of any European Court forcing clergy to do something against their conscience, some contrast the stated concern of some Church bodies about that possibility with their willingness to prevent clergy from even taking the public blessing of the union of a same-sex couple. Is the leadership of the Church being consistent in its desire to protect the conscience of some of its clergy while preventing others from exercising their consciences in a different way?

As long as there are clergy serving communities who would like to be able to offer the prayerful support of the Church to same-sex couples who wish to make that public commitment, it seems the controversy is bound to rumble on.

Story

Two members of the same sex in your congregation, each obviously deep and sincere in their Christian faith, met one another through your church and they tell you they have decided to set up home together and want to live in an openly recognised and public partnership. If they asked for a public service of blessing (or a marriage, if legislation had been passed to permit it) how would you advise your church leadership to respond?

Thought to take away

Loving your neighbour as yourself must include loving those who are different from ourselves. Official statements from the churches, while varied in their approach to gay marriage, have consistently opposed homophobia. As it seems some people are homosexual in orientation and find being in a same-sex partnership a constructive way of living, whatever is decided on the matter of gay marriage they should surely be warmly welcomed into any Christian community.

Genetic manipulation

Chris Morley

O Lord, you have searched me and known me. You know when I sit down and when I rise up; you discern my thoughts from far away. For it was you who formed my inward parts; you knit me together in my mother's womb. I praise you, for I am fearfully and wonderfully made. Wonderful are your works; that I know very well. My frame was not hidden from you when I was being made in secret, intricately woven in the depths of the earth. Your eyes beheld my unformed substance. In your book were written all the days that were formed for me when none of them as yet existed.

Psalm 139:1, 2, 13-16

Background information

Genetic manipulation is the process of altering the genetic make-up of an embryo. The aim might be to change the gender of the child or alter its susceptibility to disease, its appearance, personality, or IQ. This is illegal under current (2012) British law. Whilst few would consider it appropriate to use the techniques available to produce so-called 'designer babies', some would argue for the right to attempt to 'cure' genetic diseases in embryos by replacing faulty sections of DNA with healthy DNA. This 'germ line therapy' can be carried out on an egg, sperm or a tiny fertilised embryo. But the process is risky. New diseases may be introduced and current immunities lost. Inserting a gene to serve one purpose may cause other traits to be expressed that could be harmful to us.

Currently legal, however, under conditions supervised by the Human Fertilisation and Embryology Authority, is the screening of embryos for genetic disease: only selected embryos are implanted back into the mother's womb. The Church of England regards Pre-implantation Genetic Diagnosis (PGD) as acceptable only for conditions which are either life-threatening or involve a quality of life most people would deem unbearable. The Roman Catholic Church completely rejects such prenatal screening arguing that no embryo, such as those found wanting when screened, should be destroyed.

Sermon ideas

Every human being is made in God's image and is treasured by God. No physical or mental deformity changes this fundamental religious belief. So a child born with a genetic disorder is in no way inferior or less deserving of love and respect than anyone else.

However, though such children may well be treasured, it is human nature to wish that the suffering for them and others that such disorders often bring could have been avoided. What's more, removing suffering and bringing wholeness and healing was central to Jesus' ministry. So when medical science discovers ways of detecting in an embryo whether it will produce someone with such disorders, and sometimes ways of changing the embryo so that this danger is removed, there seems every religious and humanitarian reason to use them.

The process though prompts some fundamental questions.

Are we usurping God's prerogative if we interfere with the development of an embryo? The psalm quoted above describes God as responsible for how we are 'knit in our mother's womb'. Does this suggest we should leave the embryo as God created it? The story of the Tower of Babel (Genesis 11:1-9) describes God intervening when human beings get above themselves. Is genetic manipulation a scientific advance too far?

What might we lose? Had the embryos of people still alive been manipulated, we would probably not have had Stephen Hawkins and many others equally loved by their families.

Can we trust human nature? Discoveries in this area of medical science could be put to destructive use by a dictator, or gradually create an unjust society where human life was diminished if those with money or power chose to exploit the possibilities to their advantage. Aldous Huxley's *Brave New World* portrays a community where this has happened.

Scientific discoveries are God's gift, ways of enhancing human life and our use of the earth's creative potential. But some of them have been used instead to exploit, demean and endanger. The possibility of genetic manipulation challenges us to find ways of making appropriate use of this gift without perverting God's intentions for his world.

Story

In Aldous Huxley's book, *Brave New World*, all embryos are genetically manipulated in order to make people like the place in society to which they are destined and so create maximum happiness. Children are created, 'decanted' and raised in Hatcheries and Conditioning Centres, where they are divided into five groups.

The ruling group are the Alphas, with the Betas as their subordinates. Each of them is unique. But members of the lower castes ('Gamma', 'Delta', 'Epsilon') are subjected to chemical interference to cause arrested development in intelligence or physical growth according to their predetermined role in society.

'Alpha children wear grey. They work much harder than we do, because they're so frightfully clever. I'm awfully glad I'm a Beta, because I don't work so hard. And then we are much better than the Gammas and Deltas. Gammas are stupid. They all wear green, and Delta children wear khaki. Oh no, I don't want to play with Delta children. And Epsilons are still worse. They're too stupid to be able to read or write. Besides they wear black, which is such a beastly colour. I'm so glad I'm a Beta.'

Aldous Huxley, Brave New World, Chapter 2[13]

Thought to take away

'The time to talk about (genetic engineering) is now, in schools and churches and magazines. If you wait, five years from now the gene doctor will be hanging out the MAKE A SMARTER BABY sign down the street.'

Arthur Caplan (Time Magazine)

---

13. pp.22-3 in Vintage Books, paperback edition, London 1994.

Gluttony

Helen Costigane

You shall have no gods except me.

Deuteronomy 5:7 (Jerusalem Bible)

Background information

The sin of gluttony is often associated with the over-consumption of food, but it is more than this. It is not only related to over-indulgence, but also to an inordinate obsession with food, drink or consumption of anything to the point of waste. This can sometimes be attributed to a person trying to fill 'a hole in their soul', or as a compensation for something they believe to be lacking in their lives, such as love, affection and emotional fulfilment.

Sermon ideas

Over-consumption in itself can become a god where all we want is more. For the Christian this is problematic, firstly, in that it puts ourselves, rather than God, at the centre of our lives, and may encourage a false notion of self-sufficiency. The story of Jesus in Matthew reminds us that 'one does not live on bread alone' (Matthew 4:4), and that consumption can become a substitute for prayer and reflection. It can also be used as a shield against loneliness and isolation and a futile attempt to bolster a fragile self-image. This can lead to neglect of God and of the poor through an attitude of self-centredness and self-indulgence (Proverbs 23:20, 21; Philippians 3:19). The Christian answer to gluttony is not self-denial for its own sake but that the rhythm of feasting and enjoying food at times of celebration, and fasting at other times, reminds us that our deepest needs are met in our relationship with God.

Secondly, such conspicuous consumption of the earth's resources has implications for present and future generations, with the recognition that actions now have consequences beyond present borders and timelines. As Pope John Paul II noted in discussing the issue of consumption:

> Equally worrying is the ecological question which accompanies the problem of consumerism and which is closely connected to it. In his desire to have and to enjoy rather than to be and to grow,

> man consumes the resources of the earth and his own life in an excessive and disordered way.[14]

The remedy for this is a re-discovery of the idea of the 'common good', which attaches to national communities and that of the whole human family, and an understanding that the ecological crisis, fuelled by over-consumption, is the responsibility of everyone.[15] What is required is encapsulated in the word 'solidarity'. John Paul II says that:

> . . . in a world divided and beset by every type of conflict, the conviction is growing of a radical interdependence and consequently of the need for a solidarity which will take up interdependence and transfer it to the moral plane. Today perhaps more than in the past, people are realising that they are linked together by a common destiny, which is to be constructed together, if catastrophe for all is to be avoided.[16]

Solidarity is 'not a feeling of vague compassion or shallow distress at the misfortunes of so many people'. Rather, 'it is a firm and persevering determination to commit oneself to the common good; that is to say to the good of all and of each individual, because we are all really responsible for all.[17]

Story

A song by Shania Twain, 'Ka-Ching', expresses the problem well for our own day:

> We live in a greedy little world
> that teaches every little boy and girl
> to earn as much as they can possibly
> then turn around and spend it foolishly.
> We've created us a credit card mess.
> We spend the money that we don't possess.
> Our religion is to go and blow it all,
> so it's shoppin' every Sunday at the mall.[18]

Anyone visiting a mall at the weekend will testify to the crowds and chaos that are often part of the 'shopping experience', with parents dragging round reluctant under-fives, teenagers looking for the latest fashion fix, and young adults considering the newest techie-gadgets. The problem is that many purchases are often unaffordable, though the immediate reality is disguised by the placebo effect of the credit card.

Thought to take away

What do we need to do? Perhaps a way forward is to consider the virtue of temperance, defined as a firm disposition to moderate our desires for the sake of more important goods, and is a highly relevant ethic, as it can be used to enable us to face our patterns of consumption. This virtue can also be understood as 'restraint' or 'self-control', and one way of expressing solidarity with those suffering environmental injustice can be to consider how in our own lives we can 'reduce, reuse, or recycle' and embrace a greater simplicity of life.

Questions for each of us include the question of who is God for me, and what idols I might have set up in opposition to the true God. Furthermore, there are questions as to what my relationship with God means in terms of the way I live today, and my relationships with my national and universal community, and the planet which sustains my life.

14. John Paul II, Centesimus Annus, 1991, para. 37.
15. *The Ecological Crisis: A Common Responsibility* (Message, World Day of Peace), 1990, para. 15.
16. *Sollicitudo Rei Socialis*, 1987, para. 26.
17. *Sollicitudo Rei Socialis*, para. 38.
18. 'Ka-Ching', © Copyright John 'Mutt' Lange and Shania Twain (Mercury Records, 2002).

Gossip

Clare Richards

No human being can tame the tongue – a restless evil, full of deadly poison. With it we bless the Lord and Father, and with it we curse men, who are made in the likeness of God. From the same mouth come blessing and cursing. My brethren, this ought not to be so.

James 3:8-10 (Revised Standard Version)

Background information

It is interesting that the word gossip derives from late Old English 'God and Sibling', and was given to mean the godparent, the baptismal sponsor. Over centuries it came to mean a friend with whom you gossiped, and by the nineteenth century it shifted to imply 'idle talk'. We probably all love a good gossip with family and friends, as communication is an essential part of our human nature. However, with the advent of the internet and mobile phones, of television reality shows and the growth of celebrity culture, gossip has become more sinister in many ways. It can lead to the spread of misinformation, tittle-tattle that thrives on discussing and exaggerating scandals, and to rumour-mongering. It is no wonder that James was aware of the damage that can come from gossip.

Sermon ideas

James' writing is regarded as a sermon rather than a letter. He urges the Christian community to have nothing to do with the 'deadly poison' of malicious talk, but to use our tongues to praise God. He was repeating the warnings given by the writer of Proverbs in the Jewish scriptures. 'A gossip goes about telling secrets, but one who is trustworthy in spirit keeps a confidence' (Proverbs 11:13). 'Where there is no whisperer, quarrelling ceases' (Proverbs 26:20).

We need to reflect on these wise words as we are bombarded today with idle chat of a trivial and sometimes damaging nature, in some newspapers, magazines, and on television. Gossip is seen as entertainment for many, shown so distastefully in reality shows like *Big Brother*. We need only to turn to the internet to find celebrity gossip, football gossip, soap, showbiz and Hollywood gossip. Ethical reporters will always check facts, but some write stories that are not so committed to accuracy. Recent research shows concern about gossip on Facebook and Twitter. It is usually quite harmless but can result in bullying when victims are targeted, which in some cases has led to suicide.

This is an even greater concern with mobile and smart phones. It gives the users an illusion of intimacy, even though research has shown that most people recognise that face-to-face communication is better. Early research reported that the mobile phone has become a 'vital social lifeline' due to a 'fragmented modern world'. It concluded that gossip was not a trivial pastime, but rather 'essential to human, social, psychological and even physical well-being'. It may be a biased report, as it was commissioned by BT Cellnet.[19] Gossip affects us all, and it can do so for our good. It is healthy to keep in touch, to share and celebrate with friends. It is a way in which we can voice our concerns for the disadvantaged, the sick and all in need. This is what Christ has called us to do.

Story

Have you ever played 'Chinese Whispers' at a party or family gathering? All sit in a circle and a leader whispers a message into their neighbour's ear, which is then passed around the whole group in whispers. The resulting message can be amusing as it seldom bears any resemblance to the original one. That tells us something.

Gossip can be used to amuse us. All who watch *Coronation Street* are entertained by Norris, who serves in the local store. He takes nosy interest in peoples' lives and actions, and through tittle-tattle he delights in passing it on, often getting everything distorted. He brings a touch of humour to the programme.

There is an old saying: 'Sticks and stones can break my bones, but words will never hurt me.' This is not true!

Thought to take away

We need to be aware that none of us is immune to the damaging aspect of gossip. If we enjoy listening to gossip we are really just as much at fault as the gossip-monger. We must be careful not to repeat things we heard in confidence; we should keep that to ourselves. Remember that what we are told about others may not be completely true at all. We must never judge others. A Spanish proverb says: 'Whoever gossips to you will gossip about you.' But we should not let that be the reason for avoiding gossip. If our mind is focused on God perhaps we could make Psalm 19, verse 14, a daily prayer:

'Let the words of my mouth and the
meditation of my heart
be acceptable in thy sight,
O Lord, my rock and my redeemer.'

Revised Standard Version

---

19. Research commissioned by BT Cellnet, 2001. Summary written by Kate Fox.

Guilt

Joy Tetley

I will get up and go to my father, and I will say to him, 'Father, I have sinned against heaven and before you; I am no longer worthy to be called your son . . .'

Luke 15:18, 19

Background information

In Christian understanding, guilt serves as a gateway to grace. Its proper purpose is to lead in the direction of God's saving love, not towards condemnation and despair. It should prompt that repentance which is a turning towards God, in acknowledgement of wrong and the need for forgiveness.

Guilt, therefore, should not be an end in itself, nor a punishing cross to bear. Christ has borne that cross in a decisive way. Indeed, it is notable how, in the New Testament, so little use is made of the word 'guilt' and its associates. Repentance and grace are far more heavily emphasised. This is not to say, of course, that wrongdoing and wrong attitudes are taken lightly. 'Sin' is most definitely regarded by the New Testament writers as a serious and universal fact of life. As Paul puts it, 'All have sinned and fall short of the glory of God' (Romans 3:23).

In one way or another, we are all guilty of failing to live up to God's intended standards for us, of breaking the two great, summary commandments to love God and love one's neighbour as oneself. It is also the case that the grace of God does not render obsolete the legal framework of society or the demands of morality. In human terms, the due consequences of transgression must be faced. Paul makes it very clear that we cannot justify a life of sin by simply appealing to God's abundant grace (Romans 6:1, 2). A sense of guilt can serve to jolt us out of such opportunist complacency. It is not meant, however, to trap us in prisons of our own making or in a persistent self-condemnation which can push us into self-absorption.

Whether we are confronting guilt in an objective sense (we have been proclaimed guilty of an offence) or in the subjective sense of feeling guilty, the next stage in personal terms is to walk through the gateway of grace. Then we will discover a forgiveness which is based on the truth of the matter, and which springs from a divine love shown forth in Jesus, who 'himself bore our sins in his body on the cross' (1 Peter 2:24).

God's Calvary love offers us new beginnings and fresh hope. It is not 'cheap grace', however, for either party. For God, it costs the unimaginable experience of the Cross. From us, in thankful response, it requires that our manner of life begins to reflect God's gracious concern for the well-being of all – including those to whom we have caused offence and hurt.

Sermon ideas

In many and various ways, guilt can point us along the road to salvation. It is not meant to trap us in the clutches of destructive self-condemnation but to propel us into the arms of the God of forgiveness and grace.

Jesus brings this truth home in what is, understandably, one of his most famous parables, the one most widely known as the parable of the prodigal son (Luke 15:11-32). In this story, the son who has left home and squandered everything on dissolute living (not a phenomenon confined to the first century AD!) comes to his senses, deciding to return to his father, asking for nothing more than to be treated as one of the hired servants. At least they have the means to live. This ne'er-do-well son is now reduced to feeding pigs (regarded in his background as unclean animals) whilst he himself is on the brink of starvation. In every sense, he is wallowing in the mire. And he has clearly brought it on himself.

Here is the critical moment. At this point, he could now give himself over to guilty despair, thus, in all likelihood, completing the work of self-destruction. But there is another option. Acknowledging that he has made a mess of things, he could take the risk of asking the only one who could help if he can make some kind of fresh start. This most definitely seems to be the better option. He does not dare to presume that things could be as they were before but at least they would be better than they are now. So the young man responds to what are, in truth, the promptings of grace in the midst of his guilty condition. He is in for something of a surprise. His father has, in fact, been looking out for him and, seeing him coming 'while he was still far off', runs to meet and embrace him. Great celebrations ensue at his return to the bosom of the family.

This parable presents us with an enduring spiritual truth. Whenever guilt turns us in the direction of our heavenly Father, we shall find a welcome beyond our expectations and deserving, and a forgiveness which reaches into the depths.

But what happens next? Hopefully, for the younger son and for all those who have opened themselves to forgiveness, there is a future way of life in which God's love breeds love in them, a life in which they know their need of turning regularly to God, in penitence and faith, so that God's grace might continue to have its saving way. But the context and the conclusion of the parable also sound a warning note. The story was told in response to the grumbling of the Pharisees and scribes that Jesus was welcoming 'sinners' and eating with them. The story concludes with the anger and resentment of the respectable elder son, who cannot accept his father's gracious behaviour towards his errant brother. As he sees it, it is just not fair.

It is worth asking ourselves, therefore, how we respond to each of the sons in the parable – and what our heavenly Father might be wanting to say to us through them both.

Story

John Newton (1725-1807) is a vivid example of how guilt can be transformed by God's grace. After a troubled childhood, his life became chaotic and his behaviour dissolute. Spending much time (often far from happy) as a seafarer, he became involved in the maritime slave trade. Looking back, he describes himself during this period as 'an infidel and libertine'. His key moment of conversion came in 1748, when he cried out to God for mercy in the midst of a violent storm at sea. As he put it in the epitaph he wrote for himself, he then and thereafter found himself 'by the rich mercy of our Lord and Saviour Jesus Christ preserved, restored, pardoned . . .' In ailing old age, his memory almost gone, he still managed to say this: 'there are two things I can never forget, that I am a great sinner and that Jesus Christ is a great Saviour.'

Newton became a much-loved minister and a significant hymn-writer. His hymns are characterised by deep personal devotion and the profound impact of God's grace. One of his most popular, even to this day, comes directly out of his own experience:

Amazing grace (how sweet the sound!)
that saved a wretch like me!
I once was lost, but now am found;
was blind, but now I see.

Thought to take away

Through many dangers, toils and snares
I have already come:
'tis grace has brought me safe thus far,
and grace will lead me home.

(John Newton, Amazing grace)

Healing

Helen Warwick

Now in Jerusalem by the Sheep Gate there is a pool, called in Hebrew Bethzatha, which has five porticoes. In these lay many invalids – blind, lame, and paralysed. One man was there who had been ill for thirty-eight years. When Jesus saw him lying there and knew that he had been there a long time, he said to him, 'Do you want to be made well?' The sick man answered him, 'Sir, I have no one to put me into the pool when the water is stirred up; and while I am making my way, someone else steps down ahead of me.' Jesus said to him, 'Stand up, take your mat and walk.' At once the man was made well, and he took up his mat and began to walk.

John 5:2-9

Background information

Jesus demonstrates in this story the healing that God offers, the motivational force that changes lives. 'Brokenness and wounding do not occur in order to break human dignity but to open the heart so God can act.'[20] God offers health in mental, spiritual, physical and social areas of life; healing in various ways to meet the differing needs of each individual. The man in this story would require healing in all these areas, having spent a large majority of this time lying and waiting. Healing is part of the divine offer of wholeness, integration of these areas, restoring purpose in life and a right relationship with God the Creator.

Sermon ideas

It must have been a strange environment, these ailing people, the outcasts and unclean, lying around the colonnades waiting for the stirring of the pool. They had seen the miracles of those healed, the fortunate ones who had managed to enter the pool first, when the water was agitated by an intermittent spring, or maybe by angelic hands. What a life these people had of waiting and hoping. Jesus notices this particular man who had been enduring this life, perhaps for the longest (thirty-eight years) amongst these suffering people.

Suffering brings out differing reactions in people. Many will seek to ignore the part of themselves that seems withered or lame, trying to carry on with life remaining unaffected. Some will rebel against what they are going through. They may be angry and resentful towards God. This paralysed man became resigned – or re-signed. He was far from the path God had in mind for him; his signs were pointing to the pool of hope and to others, waiting for them to help him.

Jesus offers another way through our suffering, one that refocuses on God's path. He asks the man whether he wants to be made well. This translates from the original Greek as, 'Do you wish and will to be whole?' He offers the challenge of connecting to God within, to the motivational power of health and wholeness. To take on this challenge the man would have to pick up his mat. This is his area that marks his spot, his place of security by the pool. This is where he lays himself down, to sit inactive and wait. To accept this healing he is being asked to change his focus from the pool of hope, take up his safety mat and alter his ways. He is being asked to search deep within himself and connect to the God within, finding the courage there to move out of the place that has been his destination for many years. He will need to help himself, rather than wait for others to perform. The man takes up the challenge and obeys Jesus. It is in this act of obedience that he is healed. 'It stands to reason, doesn't it, that if the alive-and-present God who raised Jesus from the dead moves into your life, he'll do the same thing in you that he did in Jesus, bringing you alive to himself? When God lives and breathes in you (and he does, as surely as he did in Jesus), you are delivered from that dead life. With his Spirit living in you, your body will be as alive as Christ's!' (Romans 8:11, The Message).

Story

Crowhurst Christian Healing Centre offers a place of retreat and ministry near Battle, East Sussex. Its history involves the Reverend Howard Cobb who in 1925 met James Moore Hickson, an Australian layman, who had picked up his mat and come to Britain in 1905 to revive the Ministry of Healing in the Anglican Church. Howard invited James to take a mission in his church in London. Before it could take place Howard contracted sleeping sickness and was close to death. James laid hands on Howard and within the day he began to recover. During his period of convalescence Howard felt called by the Lord into the healing ministry. He was challenged to move out of his area so he advertised to exchange his London residence with someone who had a large rectory. In 1928 Howard became rector of St George's, Crowhurst, taking in guests in need of restoration and healing. In 1930 he courageously resigned as rector and with his wife, May, bought the rectory (now known as the Crowhurst Christian Healing Centre) and gave himself full-time to the work of healing.

Thought to take away

Jesus offers healing through signs that point inwards, to connect to God within, and outwards to connect to fulfilling his purpose. The paralysed man is only healed by accepting this path which entailed changing his focus, getting out of his comfort zone and having faith in Jesus. Where are your signs directed?

20. Martin Marty, *A Cry of Absence*, Harper and Row, 1983. p.123.

Human rights

Bruce Kent

Then the king will say to those at his right hand, 'Come, you that are blessed by my Father, inherit the kingdom prepared for you from the foundation of the world; for I was hungry and you gave me food, I was thirsty and you gave me something to drink, I was a stranger and you welcomed me, I was naked and you gave me clothing, I was sick and you took care of me, I was in prison and you visited me.'

Then the righteous will answer him, 'Lord when was it that we saw you hungry and gave you food, or thirsty and gave you something to drink? And when was it that we saw you a stranger and welcomed you, or naked and gave you clothing? And when was it that we saw you sick or in prison and visited you?'

And the king will answer them, 'Truly, I tell you, just as you did it to one of the least of these who are members of my family, you did it to me.'

Matthew 25:34-40

Background information

The phrase 'Human Rights' is quite a new one in human history. Some have described the current set of universal human rights as the secular version of Christian and Jewish social ethics. This is overgenerous. Until late in the nineteenth century some Christians even condoned slavery if freely entered into.

The most significant list of 'Human Rights' is in the UN Universal Declaration of 1948 which starts its first article with the ringing sentence 'All human beings are born free and equal in dignity and rights . . .'

There are echoes here of the American Bill of Rights and the French Declaration of the Rights of Man and the Citizen of 1789. The latter begins: 'Men are born free and equal in rights. These rights are liberty, property, security and resistance to oppression.'

Even though around the world many of the 'rights' listed in the 1948 Declaration represent hope rather than reality, it is a great step forward to have a yardstick by which to measure the behaviour of governments. Controversy between rich and poor countries about human rights is ongoing. The rich countries stress the individual rights of personal liberty and freedom of expression. The poorer countries emphasise collective social rights like food and health care. What is largely absent, except in the Muslim tradition, is much mention of the duties, and not just the rights, of citizens.

Sermon ideas

The phrase 'Human Rights' is not one that ever came out of the mouth of Jesus. In terms of human history it is a new arrival. The most comprehensive list of agreed human rights is to be found in the United Nations Declaration agreed in December 1948. It is called A Universal Declaration and has since been developed and expanded in many other ways.

Some rights, like the right to life, liberty and security of person in Article 3 are clearly basic. Some have always been controversial. How much right is there to 'free expression' as in Article 19? When does free expression become libel or even dangerous?

Nevertheless, the Universal Declaration is of great value to the human race. We now accept that human beings, members of one family, ought to be bound by one common rule of behaviour, even if today our words and our deeds often do not always match.

But what about Jesus? The teaching of Jesus goes far beyond any list that can be drawn up. His perspective is not the law of decent neighbourly behaviour but the spirit of unconditional love. That there is any discussion of rights at all is because we are one people and all equal children of God. As St Peter says in the Acts of the Apostles (Acts 10:35 in the Jerusalem Bible translation), 'God does not have favourites.' That means seeing God in everyone. Rights are a matter of law. Love is a matter of the spirit.

Archbishop Romero, martyred in 1980, put it this way: 'If we could see that Christ is the needy one, the torture victim, the prisoner, the murder victim, and in each human figure so shamefully thrown by our roadsides could see Christ himself cast aside, we would pick him up like a medal of gold to be kissed lovingly.'[21]

We Christians have not always had this unconditional love of others. We can regret our past collective failings, but let us not forget the heroes of unconditional love such as Elizabeth Fry, the great Quaker prison reformer, or Peter Damien who became a leper by living with lepers, or St Francis who went to meet the Muslim enemy with love – or the carer in your parish who faithfully and lovingly looks after an elderly parent or a damaged child.

Story

Some years ago in Turin, Italy, a Consolata missionary sister left her office and began to walk to church for Mass. An African woman in some distress, looking like a prostitute, came up to her and asked for help. 'Not now,' said the nun, 'see me after Mass.'

Up she went to the front of the church. Then she realised that the woman was kneeling, weeping, at the very back. The gospel story about the proud Pharisee at the front and the humble sinner at the back, came to her and she went back down the church and heard the woman's story.

So began Sister Eugenia's wonderful campaign to protect and rescue trafficked women, of whom there are many thousands, especially Africans, in Italy and the rest of Europe. Legal representation, safe houses, prosecution of traffickers, support and comfort for detainees, international arrangements to make safe return home possible – all that came out of one simple meeting and a change of heart. The human rights of one became the human rights of many.

Thought to take away

Perhaps a few words from the Venerable Nichidatsu Fujii, the founder of the Japanese Buddhist order which built the pagodas at Battersea and Milton Keynes, will keep your mind turning on human rights. In one of his last speeches he said:

'Civilisation is neither to have electric lights,
nor airplanes, nor to produce nuclear bombs.
Civilisation is not to kill man, not to destroy things,
not to make war.
Civilisation is to hold mutual affection and to respect
each other.'[22]

21. Homilies, 16 March 1980.
22. The Most Revd. Nichidatsu Fujii, *Policies for Creating a Peaceful Nation*, Hanaokayama Dōjō, Japan, October 1950.

Hunger

Jocelyn Bryan

How does God's love abide in anyone who has the world's goods and sees a brother or sister in need and yet refuses help? Little children, let us love, not in word or speech, but in truth and action.

1 John 3:17, 18

Background information

Currently in East Africa another food crisis is raging. More than 10 million people are living in areas of drought and experiencing food shortages. Hundreds of thousands have decided that their only hope is to leave their homes and search for food. Sadly, such crises like this one are not isolated events. One billion people suffer from hunger. One in seven of the world's population goes to bed hungry. Despite the immense global technical, scientific and medical progress which continues at an astonishing rate, deaths from malnutrition represent over half of the nine million deaths of children under five in the developing world. But the problem is not a global lack of food but poor distribution, wastage and rising prices. One child dies every four seconds and this could be prevented.

Hunger is not restricted to the developing world. As financial hardship spreads and the recession shows no sign of abating, there is evidence that thousands of children in the UK are not getting sufficient food. Charities working with children in London, Bristol and Barnsley are all reporting children coming to them in need of a decent meal. The School Food Trust is concerned that for many children the free school lunch is their only proper meal each day. Children are going to school too hungry to learn and fearful that they will not have any food when they get home in the evening.[23]

Sermon ideas

When Michael Buerk, the BBC reporter, revisited Ethiopia 20 years on from the time he made his shocking film of the famine which shook the world and was the catalyst for Live Aid and Band Aid, he ended his programme with these words: 'Ethiopians believe that life is a short and painful interlude to be bravely borne. The truth is that they have been betrayed; betrayed by their rulers who have been tyrants and now seem to care but are trapped by ideology and circumstance. Betrayed by us; the outside world is ashamed to let them die but has only succeeded in keeping ever-greater numbers just alive.'[24]

To be relentlessly hungry is to be just alive. But addressing hunger by keeping ever greater numbers just alive is little more than shameful. The fact that millions in our world are suffering such an existence points overwhelmingly to our failure to deal responsibly with the gifts of creation. God entrusts us with the responsibility to be stewards of creation and we have allowed personal advantage and our management of creation to be blighted by sin, injustice and suffering.

The issue of hunger is one that reveals a divided world in which the gap between poor and rich nations still remains. Yet, as Christians, we are part of a universal Church that has amongst its members many who struggle for survival in the developing world. As the body of Christ, we are called to build one another up in love and to love our neighbours as ourselves. This compels us to loving action, which has to address the inequality and injustice of the distribution of wealth and resources in the world. Charles Birch's words suggesting that the 'rich must live more simply that the poor may simply live' is a starting point but not enough.

Hunger is a politically charged issue. It requires both an individual and a corporate response. The challenge of the words in 1 John 3 summons those of us who have more than enough to repentance and to re-examine our own lifestyles and commitment to serve and love our brothers and sisters in Christ. We also need to think of new ways to change hearts and minds. The cries of the hungry must no longer go unheeded. National and international communities must work together to find solutions to overcome the world hunger problem. As Christians living in a world of greed and diminishing non-renewable natural resources, we need to draw upon God's wisdom as we respond to our responsibility as stewards of creation and our calling to love and meet the needs of our brothers and sisters.

Story

In Niger, a young woman of 14 years of age lies in hospital after the death of her baby during childbirth. Lack of food during her pregnancy and her age are the main causes of the distressing end to her pregnancy. She was married at 12 years and will try for another baby when she goes home to her village.

In northern Kenya, a mother queues for six hours for water. She will get 25 gallons which will last for 10 days for her family of eight.[25]

Tom's skin is pale, he has dark rings under his eyes. The only decent meal he can hope for during the week is his school lunch. His brother, who is no longer at school, has lost his adult teeth because his diet has been so unhealthy. They live in a tower block in London.

Thought to take away

To tackle hunger we need to act personally and corporately. This requires a re-examination of our personal lifestyles and how as church communities we can mobilise ourselves and others into action. The issue reaches to the heart of how we manage and distribute the earth's resources and what our responsibility as stewards of creation entails.

23. http://www.independent.co.uk/life-style/health-and-families/health-news/look-back-in-hunger-britains-silent-scandalous-epidemic-7622363.html. Accessed 24 July 2012.
24. http://news.bbc.co.uk/1/shared/spl/hi/programmes/correspondent/transcripts/Ethiopia%2011_01_04.txt.
25. http://www.worldhunger.org/world_hunger_pictures.htm.

Hypocrisy

Siobhán O'Keeffe

Jesus said, 'If you continue in my word, you are truly my disciples; and you will know the truth, and the truth will make you free.'

John 8:31, 32

Background information

Hypocrisy is a duplicity of thought and action. A person may express an ideal and live in a way which is very contrary to that which is expressed. They are not congruent in their actions and deceive themselves and others. Thought and behaviour are characterised by deception. Relationships are characterised by a lack of sincerity with little thought for the impact of behaviour on others. An attitude of superiority displaces humility and the person at the mercy of the hypocrite may suffer greatly. There is little place for compassion in the behaviour of the hypocrite and an attitude of self-seeking or self-glorification are common. In the story of the prodigal son (Luke 15:11-32), all of these characteristics are demonstrated in the behaviour of the elder son. By comparison, the authenticity and humility of both the father and younger son reveal to us how we may live real and authentic lives.

Sermon ideas

We all like to think of ourselves as authentic people: genuine in our relationships, honest and truthful in our dealings with others. When we consider the obituary that will be written about us these are the words that we would wish to hear. When we reflect on the gospel message of Jesus, we are challenged to ask ourselves, is this really true of us? As followers of Jesus we wish to grow in self-knowledge so that the truth will set us free.

How do we do this we may ask. In what ways do we need to change? What are the masks that we wear or the lies that we live in our daily lives? In the silence of our hearts we are invited to listen to the words of Jesus, 'the truth will set you free. Then you will indeed be my disciples.'

We are challenged to ask ourselves, do we wish to be disciples of Jesus or are the wiles of Satan and the world more appealing to our spirit?

Honest confession of our vulnerability and weakness are necessary if we are to become the people God wishes us to be. We are reminded of God's great love for us when he tells us that he loves us with an unconditional love and that he is constant in his affection for us. A deep inner knowledge of this great love will help us to choose to be ever more authentic in our daily lives as we desire to walk ever closer to our Lord and Saviour, Jesus who is the way, the truth and the life.

Story

A young woman wished to develop her career. Her parents had always taught her to be honest and truthful in her dealings with others. They had advised her to 'act justly, love tenderly and walk humbly with your God' (Micah 6:8).

Opportunities for professional development were very limited in her own country. She loved her country, kinsfolk and her father's house and wished to remain living in her homeland, if possible. However, she realised that she would not be able to obtain the training that she needed as most of the training places were taken by people who had asked politicians to reserve a place for them on the course of her choice. She did not agree with corruption and did not wish to obtain a place by foul means.

Her friends could not understand her decision and one of them said to her, 'I will speak to Mr Smith and ask him to get you a training place in a college in another part of the country.' He said, 'Everyone is using their influential friends to achieve their goals.' She declined his offer as she felt that this was not in line with the principles of the gospel, or the values that had been taught to her by her parents. She was also aware that the poor do not have influential friends to win favours for them. She always wished to stand with the voiceless and be their voice.

She felt angry that her friend wished to compromise her principles and declined the offer made to her. She made a difficult and painful decision to emigrate and follow her course of studies overseas where she secured a place on merit rather than on influence. This decision allowed her the moral freedom to follow her desire through a path of integrity.

There were many challenges in adapting to a new land but riches were manifold. God blessed her life through new encounters and she deepened her relationship with God and others. She grew in self-knowledge.

In the moments of loneliness and doubt, her parents' words, 'always be honest and truthful in your dealings with others' rang deep in her soul. Her peace was restored and she gave thanks to her parents and her God for this wisdom. She asked God for the grace to walk in the ways of the Lord each day of her life.

Thought to take away

Am I willing to pay the price that my decision to act with integrity may cause me?
Am I just and fair in my dealings with others?
Do I believe that the truth will set me free?

Islamophobia

Edgar Ruddock

God is love, and those who abide in love abide in God, and God abides in them. Love has been perfected among us in this: that we may have boldness on the day of judgement, because as he is, so are we in this world. There is no fear in love, but perfect love casts out fear; for fear has to do with punishment, and whoever fears has not reached perfection in love.

1 John 4:16-18

Background information

To understand why there is an increase of fear of Islam in the western world, we need to set the issue in a wider context.

- The increase of globalisation, modern travel and communications, and the huge increase in patterns of global migration. Change is happening at such a pace that it is very hard for emotions, mindsets, and inner personal securities to catch up with all that is happening.
- Multi-culturalism is a mixed blessing. 'Difference' becomes more important as we seek to reconnect with what makes 'us' unique or special, and from there it is an easy, and often sad jump to the conclusion that 'they' – the others – are less special, or more dangerous; more of a threat. These feelings become emphasised when difference is marked by contrasting images to do with language, dress, food, and others aspects of culture.
- In Britain the fears of 'otherness' have been exacerbated by a long tradition of being an island people, cut off from other migratory movements in history.
- Much of the immigration in the post-war period was from the (Christian) Caribbean and then from (a largely Muslim) Asia. In the former case English was a common language; in the latter case language has been a cause for division.

Sermon ideas

Experience shows that it does not help if we begin by calling on the uniqueness or rightness of one faith over against another. Rather, we might do better by following the teaching of Jesus and reaching out in love to our 'neighbours' – whoever they may be. If we begin with a model of *friendship*, a whole new world can open up. Friendship is no light matter: it has a deep theological basis, in the love of a loving God who longs for the best for all his creation, and longs for a living harmony among all its disparate parts. Friendship involves taking the initiative to cross boundaries, not just waiting for others to do that first. Friendship means learning to put ourselves into others' shoes, and see the world (and 'us') as others do.

The idea of friendship, taken seriously, then leads us on to discover that many of our deepest fears and anxieties are unfounded. Putting friendship into practice might look like this:

- Reaching out to Muslim neighbours, learning to understand the basis of their faith (and not assuming we know it);
- exploring our common Abrahamic past;
- recognising the deep respect Muslims have for Jesus as a prophet;
- discovering, with them, shared beliefs in a loving creator God;
- finding others who cherish marriage and the family as the heart of human community;
- working with others who long to see an end to war, injustice, hatred and division.

Let's remember too, that Christian fanaticism and fundamentalism can be equally dangerous and destructive as Islamic fundamentalism: neither religion teaches war and hatred, though both have been and still are guilty of promoting it by default in certain aspects.

Story

Two men from the same estate caught the same train to work every day. For years they neither acknowledged each other nor spoke when they passed. One was an Asian Muslim, the other an English Christian. Mutual suspicion kept them apart. Only when the train broke down one day, and they shared a common frustration in hours of waiting to be 'rescued', did they have something in common, and could begin a conversation around a shared experience. In time it led to a growing friendship, and ultimately to changing attitudes to each other, their backgrounds and beliefs.

Thought to take away

The challenge for us is to find that 'common experience', the point where the conversation can begin. At the end of the day, we have to recognise the fears that we all share, have the courage to hear the call of God to let go of them, and to remember above all, as the letters of John remind us, that 'perfect love casts out fear'. Let us then love one another!

Lust

Chris Morley

Now this I affirm and insist on in the Lord: you must no longer live as the Gentiles live, in the futility of their minds. They are darkened in their understanding, alienated from the life of God because of their ignorance and hardness of heart. They have lost all sensitivity and have abandoned themselves to licentiousness, greedy to practise every kind of impurity. That is not the way you learned Christ! For surely you have heard about him and were taught in him, as truth is in Jesus. You were taught to put away your former way of life, your old self, corrupted and deluded by its lusts, and to be renewed in the spirit of your minds, and to clothe yourselves according to the likeness of God in true righteousness and holiness.

Ephesians 4:17-24

Background information

The word lust can mean desire for power, money, knowledge or life itself – a lust for life. The contemporary linking of the word specifically with illicit strong sexual desire is first seen in early translations into English of Jesus' comment about committing adultery in the heart (Matthew 5:28). Having been used to describe a feeling equivalent to adultery, lust acquired a primarily sexual connotation.

Lust is a disordered desire for sexual pleasure, where sexual pleasure is sought for itself without deeper feelings of love and respect and any signs of reciprocation.

Spontaneous involuntary sexual thoughts aren't sinful. The Catholic Catechism says that 'In themselves passions are neither good nor evil' (Clause 1767). The sin of lust occurs when one intentionally initiates and continues to fantasise about another person in a lustfully sexual way.

Lust is one of the traditional seven deadly sins. In Catholic tradition, it is described as a capital sin, that is, a sin seen as the origin ('capital' from the Latin *caput,* head) of other sins. When acted on, lust can lead to relationships which are dishonest, manipulative and selfish.

Sermon ideas

Sexual attraction is one of God's gifts. Indeed it contributes to the way the human species propagates itself. It's often what initially brings together couples who develop a love for each other that lasts a lifetime.

Such attraction becomes lust when the one experiencing it is already married; or desires someone who is; or has no intention of allowing the relationship to develop a commitment; or sees the other not as a person, but as a sexual object, there to meet their needs. Such feelings don't have to be acted on to be sinful. Jesus condemned lustful thoughts as well as actions (Matthew 5:28).

Such thoughts can be addictive because lustful thoughts are exciting. They produce chemical reactions in the body which stimulate a feeling of being alive, of heightened awareness. Especially for anyone experiencing in their lives emptiness and boredom (and such people are particularly prone to lustful behaviour), this seems like a panacea. But there are much more appropriate sources for such feelings of alertness and well-being. A healthy well-balanced life achieves the same result, especially when accompanied by a Christian faith. Indeed the lack of a relationship with God ('alienation from the life of God') is seen by the apostle Paul in the passage quoted above as a reason why people are attracted by what he calls licentiousness.

He also suggests there that people caught up in lustful thinking and behaving often stop thinking rationally. Paul describes this as a 'darkening in their understanding'. Strong sexual feelings can de-activate a person's capacity to think and behave rationally and lead them into actions which they subsequently regret.

According to Paul, such experiences will not befall those who have been 'renewed in the spirit of (their) minds, and (have clothed themselves) according to the likeness of God'. Those who fully accept the way of Christ are unlikely to be tempted by lust because they are less likely to have the emotional needs lust seems to meet. Even if they are, Christ's Spirit in their minds will help them stop themselves from being carried away by their feelings.

Story

In *Inferno,* the first part of Dante's *Divine Comedy,* Dante and Virgil travel through Hell and are shown the punishment meted out for sins committed while on earth. Each punishment fits the crime. Those overcome by lust, who Dante calls 'carnal malefactors' have let their appetites blow away their reason. So these souls are blown to and fro by the terrible winds of a violent storm, without hope of rest.

> The infernal hurricane that never rests
> hurtles the spirits onward in its plundering[26];
> whirling them round, and smiting, it molests them.
> When they arrive before the precipice,
> there are the shrieks, the plaints, and the laments . . .
> I understood that unto such a torment
> the carnal malefactors were condemned
> who reason subjugate to appetite.
>
> *Canto V*

Thought to take away

The Catholic Catechism defines lust as 'disordered desire for or inordinate enjoyment of sexual pleasure' (Clause 2351). Its opposite is chastity. Chaste people, it says, maintain the integrity of the powers of life and love they've been given and tolerate neither a double life nor duplicity in speech. It goes on to say that chastity offers a clear alternative: either we govern our passions and find peace, or we let ourselves be dominated by them and become unhappy. Self-mastery is what we're after and human dignity involves acting out of conscious and free choice, as moved and drawn in a personal way from within, and not by blind impulses. (See Clause 2338-9.)

26. This is the most common translation, by Henry Wadsworth Longfellow, but I've here substituted the word 'plundering' for his word 'rapine'.

Lying

Deborah Jones

For the word of God is living and active, sharper than any two-edged sword . . . discerning the thoughts and intention of the heart. And before him no creature is hidden, but all are open and laid bare to the eyes of him with whom we have to do.

Hebrews 4:12, 13 (Revised Standard Version)

Background information

There are several degrees of lying, from the harmless little 'white lie', to protect the other's feelings, to the serious intention to deceive someone who has the right to know the truth. The worst is perjury, perverting the course of justice by lying under oath. Flattery, boasting, malicious sarcasm: these too can prevent real communication between people, for that depends above all on the words we use meaning what they say. We need to be on our guard not to let unworthy reasons motivate us to slip from truth-telling, for lying can easily become habitual.

Sermon ideas

Words have power. In Scripture we read that the word uttered from God's mouth brought all of creation into being. The prophets who spoke God's word were believed to bring about the benefits or calamities that they foretold, through their blessing or curse. Words can stir people into action, and soothe their fears. Words can inspire and can crush. We rely on words having a meaning that we all agree upon, otherwise we could not make sense of whatever we hear or read. We would learn nothing and trust no one. So word and meaning must be combined. Lies separate the two, irrevocably.

Just as God's Word became flesh, embodying goodness and truth, so we can also communicate through being the sort of person we are. Who we are, the way we lead our lives, and what we say and do, should be all of a piece. That is what having integrity means. The occasional casual lie, to avoid blame or exaggerate achievement, may seem very little, but a crack has opened up between the truth and the speaker, between word and meaning. That fissure can widen into an unbridgeable abyss once lying becomes commonplace and habitual. It is widely considered a matter of grave dishonour when one deliberately misleads another because all of social interaction depends on honest and fair dealing.

Sometimes we are called upon to make a solemn vow before God, in marriage, in being a godparent, or in renewing our baptism promises. To utter the words while detaching ourselves from their implications; in other words, to say 'I do' or whatever, while inwardly thinking 'I may' or even 'some chance' makes us liars of the worst sort. Trying to fool God, who is the Truth, is futile. As the psalmist exclaims 'you [God] discern my thoughts from far away . . . Even before a word is on my tongue, O Lord, you know it completely' (Psalm 139:2, 4). Again, as in the letter to the Hebrews, it is noted that we creatures are all open and laid bare to the eyes of the Creator-Word.

Story

In the 1997 film, *Liar Liar,* Fletcher, the character played by Jim Carrey is a successful and ambitious lawyer who lies both in court and at home, breaking promises and then covering his tracks. His disappointed young son wishes his father would resist from lies for a whole day – which miraculously he does. Of course the consequences in this comedy are amusing, and it appears at first that the compulsion to tell the truth risks Fletcher's career. The film, however, ends with his realising that values other than material success really matter, such as basing relationships on honesty and sincerity. He is finally reconciled with his estranged family.

Thought to take away

We cannot fool God, and we dare not corrupt relationships by choosing the way of falsehood. Whatever we say and do, whatever the personal consequences, needs to be imbued with honesty and integrity or else we estrange ourselves both from the source of all truth and from the company of other people on whom we depend. For once trust is lost, it is not easily restored. As *The Talmud,* the book of Jewish learning and wisdom, puts it: 'This is the punishment of a liar: he is not believed, even when he is telling the truth.'

Magic

Deborah Jones

There shall not be found among you . . . any one who practises divination, a soothsayer or an augur, or a sorcerer, or a charmer, or a medium, or a wizard, or a necromancer. For whoever does these things is an abomination to the Lord.

Deuteronomy 18:10-12 (Revised Standard Version)

Background information

'That's magic!' has become just another youthful term for expressing admiration. Another use of the term 'magic' is to describe the seemingly inexplicable ability of conjurers who produce rabbits out of hats, or appear to saw their assistants in half.

There is so much popular fiction, even by Christian writers such as C.S. Lewis and J.R.R. Tolkein, featuring the often benign use of magic that many people fail to see the dangers, and not only to Christians. The worst involves the invocation of demonic powers to harm one's enemy or to gain unlawful power over others. There are even websites which sell spells and curses of black magic. For example, one advertises itself by asking if the reader knows 'someone out there who deserves their comeuppance? Are you tired of being the victim and want to fight back?' It then offers the services of a 'Master in Black Magic' who 'can cast a spell to help you even the score!'

Sermon ideas

There is nothing positive about magic, despite attractive features in much popular fiction. Proponents of fictional magic use it merely as a device to drive plots that are beyond real capacities in normal life. It allows for a wildly imaginative alternative reality. They neglect to issue a health warning that magic practices can actually be hideously destructive. At the worst, some magic practices, for example in Africa, have been found to involve the torture to death of children who are believed to harbour evil spirits. In some cultures even the threat of being cursed is enough to frighten the victim to death. Magic involves invoking spirits and satanic powers, often with the intention of harming others or gaining power over them. This runs exactly counter to the Christian message of loving one's enemies and doing good to those who harm us. Scripture expressly forbids us to venture into the realm of spirits – the Holy Spirit alone should be sufficient for us.

Most Christians would not entertain the use of such magic processes as spells, incantations and the like. Yet it is all too easy to dismiss those who believe in them as gullible while at the same time indulging ourselves in a range of relatively mild superstitions, such as knocking on wood, throwing salt over one's shoulder, carrying a 'lucky' charm or other such nonsense. Whatever the ancient origins of these, pagan or Christian, their meanings have been forgotten long ago.

Other popular activities under the general heading of magic include various forms of divination, such as consulting horoscopes, engaging in astrology, clairvoyance or necromancy, interpreting omens and attending seances with mediums or Ouija boards. It is not for us to know the future; that lies in God's hands alone. And God's wisdom is sufficient for our guidance. Our prayers are for God's will to be done.

Story

In the well known 1942 standard 'That Old Black Magic' covered by many famous singers, the magic here is that of love – something that has its victim 'in its spell', imprisoned by its power. True love is like magic – inexplicable, beyond reason and compulsive. But belief in magic really does hold its victims in its mental grip, destroying not only mind and will, but often life itself. Unlike certain chocolates, there is nothing 'naughty but nice' about it.

Thought to take away

God's power cannot be manipulated by creatures. Incantations, spells, charms – or even promises of effective outcomes from the use of certain prayers – none of these has the slightest effect on God, although they may corrupt us into thinking that we can have the power to oblige God to act upon them. We pray only that God's will, not ours, be done. All spirits and their supposed powers are to be shunned. God's Spirit alone enables us to open our lives and hearts to doing God's will. Where the God of love reigns, there is no space for superstition and magic.

Materialism

John Saxbee

Then he called the people to him, as well as his disciples, and said to them, 'anyone who wants to be a follower of mine must renounce self; he must take up his cross and follow me. Whoever wants to save his life will lose it, but whoever loses his life for my sake and for the gospel's will save it. What does anyone gain by winning the whole world at the cost of his life? What can he give to buy his life back?

Mark 8:34-37 (Revised English Bible)

Background information

It is commonplace to talk about ours being a materialist culture. An emphasis is placed on accumulating possessions, and status depends upon those possessions being as up to date as possible. Current environmental concerns have alerted us to the fact that the planet as a whole pays a high price for rampant materialism in the wealthiest countries and, of course, it is those who have least who suffer most from pollution consequent upon excessive consumption. As long ago as the 1970s, Bishop John Taylor published *Enough is Enough* and since the dawn of civilisation prophetic voices have warned against sacrificing our spiritual well-being on the altar of materialism. We live in a material world, and God loves the world God has made. The Incarnation underlines that material existence is not incompatible with what is divine. But Christianity teaches that whilst material things matter, they must never matter most because there is always more than mere matter to be known, experienced and celebrated.

Sermon ideas

What is really real? The easy answer is that those things are real which we can see and touch – the things which confront us in the world day by day. But are such things *really* real? Do they have a value which transcends what they do or what they are made of or how much they cost to buy? Things which have no value other than their material worth may be real in a very limited and physical sense, but if they lack spiritual value by failing to point beyond themselves to something more precious and enduring, then they are not *really* real.

Jesus was at great pains to warn us against becoming dependent upon material things, and so putting at risk our spiritual health and even our eternal salvation. He himself seems to have had few possessions and made no effort to accumulate wealth by his teaching and healing, even though that was the usual thing to do at the time. But neither did he begrudge others their wealth and comfortable lifestyle. Rather, he challenged those like the rich man who had allowed his wealth to come between him and the claims of God on his life (Mark 10:17-22). Like money, materialism is not itself the root of all evil, but love of material things to the exclusion of love for God and neighbour most certainly is.

Materialism as a way of life requires us to deny the significance, or even the very existence, of a realm which transcends physical things – the realm of the really real. We can access that realm only when we acknowledge the secondary significance of material things in order to give priority in our lives to spiritual values such as faith and hope and love. These spiritual values may well be given material expression as in our Sacraments, and they will certainly determine the premium we place on material things in our lives. But above all they will put into perspective the physical world around us and help us to focus on what really matters, what is really real.

As human beings become more and more masters of the material world, in an age of extraordinary scientific and technological advances, we need to be all the more attentive to things of the spirit lest we do indeed win the whole world at the expense of what Jesus came to bring: life, and life in all its fullness (John 10:10).

Story

A small boy sees a coin inside a beautiful antique vase. He forces his hand through the narrow neck of the vase to grasp the coin, but with his fist clenched his hand is stuck and eventually the vase has to be smashed in order to release him. For the sake of holding on to a brass farthing, a priceless work of art has been lost for ever. It was likewise with the woman on the Titanic who is reputed to have hung on to her precious jewellery box rather than let go of it in order to take a hand held out to rescue her.

Thought to take away

Once we have adequately fed and clothed and housed every person on planet Earth, what more might they and we need to realise our full potential as made in the image of God? It is the answer to that question which takes us beyond materialism into a dimension where, indeed, not everything that matters can be measured, not everything that counts can be counted, and not everything that is valuable can be valued at a price. When that realm is realised in our own experience, then everything else becomes, well, immaterial.

Money

Paul Cox

The love of money is a root of all kinds of evil.

1 Timothy 6:10 (New International Version)

Though your riches increase, do not set your heart on them.

Psalm 62:10 (New International Version)

Background information

Money developed as communities grew and developed economic interactions over greater distances. Bartering no longer provided a flexible enough system as labour, and therefore production of goods and services, became more specialised. Forms of money have varied greatly between cultures and over time, each showing that money is the ownership of wealth in accepted ways. At one extreme there is money in the form of the transference of rights to large immovable stones in some Polynesian economies, at the other there are the pieces of plastic used in the modern banking world. Money may have intrinsic value (gold coinage) or be a promise that is confidently expected to be backed by something of real value, as in the case of our paper money and the Bank of England's chief cashier's statement, 'I promise to pay the bearer on demand the sum of . . .'). Money is largely a grand confidence 'trick' that lubricates the trading activities of economic systems. It may be, but is not necessarily, the same thing as wealth.

The link between money and wealth, and between the possession of money and its use through the power it can exercise, has meant that the acquisition of money and its ownership have reflected such contrasting sides of human nature as greed and generosity. In the complexities of the modern banking world greed has led to the near collapse of the banking system and generosity has meant the eradication of polio in all but three countries of the world.[27]

The value of money in modern western economies is not a matter of the number of units a particular coin or note represents, e.g. 5, 10, 20 or 50 pounds, but the level of labour involved in gaining such money or in the production of what can be bought with it. Thus a daily wage of £1 in a 'poor' economy may be sufficient to meet a household's daily needs of food, clothing and housing, whereas in the UK a daily wage of £50 is considered to be below the poverty level for a household of two adults and two infants.[28] A television bought in 1960 at £80 was more expensive in real terms than one of the same size bought today for £150. At times of inflation the rapid printing of money has led to notes with huge face value but with little buying power. Such hyperinflation was experienced in Germany in the 1920s and in Zimbabwe between 2006 and 2009, since when the latter has abandoned its own currency.

Sermon ideas

Money is morally neutral. We could misquote Shakespeare and say that 'In money, there is nothing good or bad but thinking makes it so' (Hamlet). That is what the statement from the letter to Timothy is saying. It is the *love* of money that is a root of all evil. But it is a malicious love. It engenders vices and sins such as greed and envy, jealousy and murder. A love of money generates possessiveness and acquisitiveness but can also lead to people themselves becoming possessed by it.

It is easy to show what can be wrong about our attitude towards money and where that leads us. Not only is there the example of mismanagement on a large scale, as shown by the banking crisis, we can also see it in the lives of individuals. Families may be caught up in feuds over disputed inheritance; divorces can be described as being 'nasty' because of disagreement over the allocation of money; children may be neglected as both parents work ever longer hours to increase their money income to obtain more 'wants', although already having sufficient to meet their needs.

The love of money can distort priorities. The Christian faith has much to say about getting our priorities right – in our relationship with God and with other people. The Church's teaching about money is based on proper stewardship. How do we prioritise the money we have? Do we give to God and his mission and ministry what change we have left over after spending on our own needs and wants, or do we allocate some money for God as a first priority? Do we try to build up our treasures by the accumulation of possessions? Jesus warns us against this: 'Do not store up for yourselves treasures on earth, where moth and rust consume, and where thieves break in and steal; but store up for yourselves treasures in heaven, where neither moth nor rust consumes and where thieves do not break in and steal. For where your treasure is, there your heart will be also' (Matthew 6:19-21).

Giving is a virtue, more blessed than receiving, and many find that in their giving, even of small monetary amounts, they indeed receive much. Churches that are generous in their giving are usually found to be 'receiving' churches. The generosity experienced by St Paul came from the church at Philippi: 'Moreover, as you Philippians know, in the early days of your acquaintance with the gospel, when I set out from Macedonia, not one church shared with me in the matter of giving and receiving, except you only; for even when I was in Thessalonica, you sent me aid again and again when I was in need' (Philippians 4:15, 16, NIV). In our own time some churches that have the funds are helping poorer churches in meeting their costs – each are finding this a blessing.

Being generous with our money is only one way of showing generosity. We can be generous in many ways. Parents and teachers, coaches and trainers all aim to share from what they have in order that others may grow in knowledge and skills and so have a better 'life', which may mean being better paid and having more money to meet their needs.

We need to be careful about what we believe God thinks about money. In Jesus' time it was thought that being well-off was a sign that God had blessed the person. Poverty would then be construed as God showing his displeasure.

Story

In many towns and cities we are likely to come across a busker, hoping that someone will give him a coin. On one occasion Paganini, a world famous violinist, was walking along a Parisian street when he came across a poor man busking, scraping a miserable tune on a cheap violin. None of the passers-by gave him any money. Paganini found that he did not have a coin on him. He paused, and then stepping into the gutter alongside the old man, smiled and gently took the violin and bow from him, and began to play. The music that was now heard was exquisite and soon people were spreading the news that it was Paganini playing. After some ten minutes Paganini told the old man to pass his hat round the crowd. He did so and met with a generous response. Paganini continued to play for a little longer, and then, handing back the violin and bow to the old man, he continued on his way.[29]

Thought to take away

A human being has a natural desire to have more of a good thing than he needs. *Mark Twain*

---

27. This has been accomplished through the generosity of Bill Gates and Rotary International.
28. UK Household Below Average Income 2009/2010 Government statistics.
29. Adapted from a story quoted in *Acts of Worship for Assemblies Vol. 3* by R. H. Lloyd (Mowbray, 1986).

Multiculturalism

Edgar Ruddock

Do not call anything impure that God has made clean!

Acts 10:15 (New International Version)

Background information

Take a walk through the inner suburbs of any of our great cities. Shops, pedestrians, signboards, homes and parks will all quickly reveal people and cultures from all around the world. Usually they will be getting along just fine, but occasionally they will reveal tensions and conflicts, fears and misunderstandings that lie just below the surface. We are all living in a fast-changing world, and sometimes our hearts and emotions don't quite catch up with the reality of what our eyes and ears are telling us is going on.

Historically, no race or culture can ever be defined as pure. Since the beginning of time, communities have been on the move, encountering one another, struggling and then settling, marrying and inter-marrying. Migrations have always happened, with more or less rapidity, and new identities emerge out of the interactions that come in their wake. Language grows and changes, taking in new ideas and understandings, and out of them come progress and development. Notice, for example, the impact on language of youth culture, the use of text messages, Facebook, Twitter etc.

Sermon ideas

The early Christians lived in a multicultural world – and struggled with it. The history of the Jews was a struggle to define identity for a people constantly encountering others, suffering conquests and defeats, taking land, and then finding it taken from them. Part of their response was a defensiveness that was expressed in their religious laws of purity, ritual cleanness, and dogmatic beliefs about being a chosen people. Another part of their heritage was a vision that the God they served was a God for all people, a God who lived and worked with all and through all.

Peter's dream was shocking because it forced him to consider his own limited world view: everything he had taken for granted about his own identity as a Palestinian Jew was threatened as the dream suggested the Good News of Jesus was for everyone, not just for a chosen few.

The implications of this insight were revolutionary. It drove the early Church out into the wider world, with a message of the inclusive love of God. The story of the New Testament, and the early Church, indicated that this lesson was a hard one to learn, that conflicts and misunderstandings are never resolved overnight.

But the opportunities presenting themselves to the Church worldwide today to be a beacon of welcome and hope for all, are myriad.

Story

Churches in our inner cities are learning to become centres of welcome for all. Places of hospitality, where strangers can meet, where difference can be celebrated, where food can be shared, songs and dances discovered, memories recalled, and hopes captured. Our confidence in our core identity – loved by God and baptised in Christ – enables us to have the energy and imagination to reach out to others, to find, and be found by them.

Many church and community groups have discovered that the sharing of food is a great way to get into an understanding of multiculturalism! The Woking People of Faith Group, for example, have been discovering that learning new tastes, discovering new vegetables, exploring new recipes and ways of cooking take us close to the heart of our own lives, and open us to the hearts of others. We discover a common fascination with food, and in its celebration and sharing. We discover hospitality. And we realise we are also discovering one another.

Thought to take away

Families are about each member being themselves and contributing to the whole. We don't expect each member to be the same – in fact we celebrate difference, often with a wry smile – Did those two really come out of the same stable?!'

Learning to live multiculturally becomes a window into heaven, into the richness and diversity of God's creative energy: each made in God's image; each uniquely gifted to reveal something of God's character that no one else can.

If that is true, we dare not be anything less than active multiculturalists. Otherwise our God is a lesser God than we thought!

Natural disasters

John Cox

In the six-hundredth year of Noah's life, in the second month, on the seventeenth day of the month, on that day all the fountains of the great deep burst forth, and the windows of the heavens were opened. The rain fell on the earth for forty days and forty nights. The flood continued for forty days on the earth; and the waters increased, and bore up the ark, and it rose high above the earth. The waters swelled and increased greatly on the earth; and the ark floated on the face of the waters. The waters swelled so mightily on the earth that all the high mountains under the whole heaven were covered; the waters swelled above the mountains, covering them fifteen cubits deep. And all flesh died that moved on the earth, birds, domestic animals, wild animals, all swarming creatures that swarm on the earth, and all human beings; everything on dry land in whose nostrils was the breath of life died. He blotted out every living thing that was on the face of the ground, human beings and animals and creeping things and birds of the air; they were blotted out from the earth. Only Noah was left, and those that were with him in the ark. And the waters swelled on the earth for one hundred and fifty days.

Genesis 7:11, 12, 17-24

Background information

On the EarthSky website Matt Daniel suggested that 2011 was a particularly bad year for natural disasters. Among the top five, he mentions the tornado that destroyed the city of Joplin. It was the worst tornado to hit the USA since modern records have been kept and the seventh deadliest of all time. 158 people died and the insurance cost was nearly three billion dollars. During June and July extreme drought hit a large area across Kenya, Somalia, Ethiopia, Eritrea and Djibouti. The United Nations declared parts of southern Somalia to be official famine zones. During the summer, nearly three million Somalis were in need of medical assistance. It is estimated that nearly 30,000 children died because of the famine. Top of Matt Daniel's list was the earthquake that hit Japan with its subsequent tsunami. The earthquake measured 8.9 on the Richter Scale and was the fifth most powerful ever recorded. It occurred six miles below the surface of the earth. It was 160 times more powerful than the earthquake that hit Christchurch, New Zealand in February 2011 and, together with the tsunami that followed it, resulted in the deaths of 15,000 people.

Sermon ideas

Insurance policies used to avoid the payment of compensation for loss or damage as a result of natural disasters by designating them as 'acts of God'. As such they were uninsurable. As a result of the severe floods in Queensland during the end of 2010 and the beginning of 2011, the Australian government called for a review of flood insurance. While storm could be insured against, flood could not. Around half a million homes in Australia are subject to flooding.

The Bible takes a similar view on natural disasters – they are acts of God. In the Scriptures nature is not only part of the created order but is under the direct control of God. It was perceived as his agent for reward and punishment. Thus those who were righteous and faithful were fruitful in their families and in their fields. Nature was not merely benign, it was positively benevolent as a direct result of a good relationship with the Lord. Those who were disobedient and evil, whether individuals or nations, could expect the wrath of God to descend on them through natural disaster. Women, flocks and herds were made barren and the forces of nature were turned against the wrongdoers. Cities were destroyed by earthquake or volcanic activity (fire and brimstone), bad rulers brought plague upon their people (Pharoah in Egypt). Most disastrous of all was the destruction of all living things through the Flood. Only the pious Noah and his family and a few representative creatures survived. So awful was it that God vowed never to exact such devastation again and gave the sign of the rainbow as a signal of this promise (Genesis 9:8-17).

The account of the storm that battered the ship carrying St Paul from Crete to Italy takes a generally neutral moral position but in the context of the whole narrative, the event of the shipwreck is seen as the occasion for God's activity in his special care of St Paul, since no one was lost (Acts 27).

When the tsunami hit the Philippines in December 2004 it was suggested by some Asian commentators that it was the result of people falling under the spell of western decadence. The disaster was a direct result of moral failure. Such views should not be dismissed too lightly. The droughts of recent years in sub-Saharan Africa, increasing and damaging tornado activity in the eastern states of the USA, and floods in Australia have been linked by some to global warming which itself is generally understood to be the result of human activity and a failure in proper stewardship of the planet.

But more generally natural disasters are explained without recourse to spiritual or moral reasons. The forces governing climate and geological activity are sufficiently understood to give 'natural' explanations for what happens. The earth is behaving as the earth should. That its activity occasionally results in tragedy is, at least in part, simply evidence of the fact that humanity does not have total control over nature. The shifting of the earth's crust, which has created the continents as we know them and produced beautiful landscapes, does not stop because we happen to get in the way. Volcanic action has ensured that the rich mineral resources of the earth have been replenished. The same action can result in loss of life and homes when people live near volcanoes.

The God who created and sustains his creation does not suddenly act to make such things happen and prayer to God will not prevent them happening. The way the world is, is the way God intended it to be and he doesn't keep interfering with the way it works. That can sound callous but it reflects the belief that God knew what he was up to in his creation. It is the arena for our development, not just as physical beings but as people called to be morally responsible and spiritually mature. Our development as people seems to require the possibility of suffering as well as comfort. Faith suggests that that is why God made the world the way it is, even though it can cause tragedy as well as be wonderfully productive and beautiful.

Story

The sea wall in Rikuzentakata was destroyed by the Japanese tsunami of March 2011, and a year later more than 3,000 people were still missing from the town. Families continued to search for bodies along the coast, hopeful that they would be able to give their loved ones a proper burial. Behind the new sea wall there stands a lone tree. It is the only survivor of a pine forest that was destroyed by the wave. It has become a national symbol of resilience and hope.[30]

Thought to take away

The Christian faith has never suggested we are kept from tragedy and disaster. It does say we are never alone as we face them and by God's grace we can learn from them both individually and as nations.

30. As reported by Roland Buerk, BBC News, 11 March 2012.

Old age

Bruce Kent

O God, from my youth you have taught me,
and I still proclaim your wondrous deeds.
So even to old age and grey hairs,
O God, do not forsake me,
until I proclaim your might
to all the generations to come.

Psalm 71:17, 18

Background information

That people in the United Kingdom and elsewhere in the richer parts of the world are living longer ought to be no surprise. On the whole we do not suffer the same health problems or food shortages experienced in poorer parts of the world. The 2011 census revealed that we in the UK have a population of about 63 million people and 10 million are 65 or over. This represents 15.7 per cent of the population. By 2020 about 10 per cent will not just be over 65 but over 75.

This is not a disaster. Older people can and do contribute in all sorts of ways to the good of the whole community. Every parish knows how much it depends on the faithful work and witness of older parishioners. Every young family knows how wonderful it is to be able to call on a grandmother or grandfather for help, especially but not only, with the children. That there are weaknesses and mobility problems as we get older is no cause for alarm. If we live as the community that God expects, then the elderly who need help can be given it. That's just payback time for those who have contributed so much to the community when they were younger.

Sermon ideas

There is an old story about a headmasters' gathering of some top single-sex public schools. Each did a bit of boasting. 'I prepare my boys for the Foreign Office.' 'Mine go into Parliament.' 'I've got one who runs Rolls Royce.'

One of the heads was a Benedictine monk from a major Catholic school. The others turned to him eventually when he was silent and asked him what he was preparing his boys for. 'Death' was his one word answer. That killed further conversation.

In one way it was a good answer and far more significant than anything on offer from anyone else. But it's only half the story. Christianity is not just a matter of waiting for the grim reaper to turn up. It is about living life as it was meant to be lived: creative, caring, imaginative, inventive and compassionate.

Parishes do not create enough opportunities to talk about getting older. To discuss how to get ready, spiritually and practically, for what we are all going to face makes sense. Too often as a parish priest, I came across situations in which the 'dear departed' had never even made practical preparations, let alone spiritual ones. A will can't be found and the family is thrown into confusion and even conflict. Insurance policies have gone missing and the surviving partner cannot get the help they need. In that sense we ought all to get ready.

But let's not get morbid. At 65 life is not over. Every year brings new opportunities. The need for volunteers grows ever greater. Jesus said that he came not just to give us life but to give it 'more abundantly'. We are meant to use our talents at any age, not to put them on a shelf.

Face up to death by all means but don't give up on life as a consequence.

Story

I remember Lord Fenner Brockway very well. His statue stands in Red Lion Square with one arm up in the air, as it often was when he made one of his impassioned speeches for social justice. As a young man he had opposed the First World War and went to prison as a result.

When he was 99 he asked me to come to see him. He had plans. He wanted there to be a major peace conference the following year. 'And I,' said he, 'will be one of the major speakers.' God must have heard this outburst of overconfidence because Fenner never made it to his 100th. But what a wonderful example of not giving up.

Age is not the issue. Determination is.

Thought to take away

One of our home-grown English mystics is Julian of Norwich, an anchorite who lived through turbulent times, which included the Peasants' Revolt of 1381. A statue of her stands today outside Norwich Cathedral. Her message, the result of visions she had when very ill, is one of the love, not the wrath of God.

Whenever I have to send a sympathy card to someone who has lost a dear friend or relation, I always use a card from the Julian shrine in Norwich which has on it her moving words:

From him we come,
in him we are enfolded,
to him we return.

Enfolded in Love –
Daily Readings with Julian of Norwich (DLT, 1980) p.32

Old age is no surprise and nor should death be. We are going home.

Organ transplant

Siobhán O'Keeffe

This is my commandment, that you love one another as I have loved you.

John 15:12

Background information

Organ donation is the donation of biological tissue or an organ of the human body from a living or dead person to a living recipient in need of a transplantation.

It is implied that there is grave reason for this procedure to take place. It is not entered into without much serious thought, reflection and consultation with the donor's family, the recipient's family and medical personnel. The preservation and upholding of good quality life is a key principle and has to be upheld at all times. This is in line with gospel principles where Jesus laid down his life for his friends. He asks us to be selfless in our care and support of each other. The confidentiality of the donor and recipient is upheld in all organ or tissue donation.

It is recognised that in the event of an organ transplant being necessary, parents or siblings are more likely to have a compatible tissue match than that which is available from another person.

Sermon ideas

'This is my commandment, that you love one another as I have loved you' (John 15:12).

This scripture is indeed pertinent, when one considers the self-gift that is made by a person donating tissue or organ for transplantation.

As members of Christ's Body we share a deep personal relationship with him and a duty of care to each other. Love one another as I have loved you is his great commission to us. Jesus invites us to share in his mission to bring the healing, liberating and empowering love of God to others. This *missio Deo* is fleshed out when one makes oneself available for organ donation. In this act of genuine generosity, hope is offered to an ill person whose quality of life is greatly compromised by organ failure. Anxiety and fear of an unknown future have robbed the ill person of joy and their human spirit may feel crushed and sore when they live beneath the shadow of organ failure. However, when the human spirit of another is moved to offer an organ, the opportunity for order to rule over chaos and life over death is made available to the person who has shared in the cross of the Master. Hope is restored, and fullness of life may once again flow through the veins of a fellow traveller.

As you listen to the following story you may wish to ask yourself: What would my response be if faced with a similar challenge? What needs to change in my life so that I can respond with greater love to the challenges that come my way each day? What is my attitude and response to organ donation issues? What may help me to respond more generously in this area of life?

Story

Following a recent kidney infection, a young man was informed by his doctor of his need for a kidney transplant. On learning that the most likely compatible match rested within the family, he asked his dad if he would be willing to donate a kidney to him. He had never doubted his father's great love for him and knew that his father would always act in his best interest as far as he was able. He acknowledged the magnitude of the request and the sense of shock that the whole family would experience on learning of the gravity of his illness and the need for transplant. He was aware that much thought, reflection and honest communication within the family were necessary before a decision could be reached. He expressed his deep gratitude to his father for his unconditional love of him. He trusted that the right decision would be made and that he would receive all the care that he needed from his family and medical team.

Thought to take away

How generous am I in my response to the needs of others?

Do I believe in God's unconditional love for me?

Is my name on the National Organ Donor register or have I asked to have it removed?

Pain

Helen Warwick

Beloved, do not be surprised at the fiery ordeal that is taking place among you to test you, as though something strange were happening to you. But rejoice in so far as you are sharing Christ's sufferings, so that you may also be glad and shout for joy when his glory is revealed.

1 Peter 4:12, 13

Background information

From the time Adam and Eve disobeyed God in the Garden of Eden and ate the fruit from the tree of good and evil, toil, pain, shame and suffering have been noted throughout the Bible. The first book of Peter has many references to the suffering that followers of Christ will go through.

Jesus reflected the fulfilled life that God offers and this included going through pain. Following God does not exempt Christians from suffering. Pain can be mental and emotional, as well as physical. Jesus suffered in all these areas and showed compassion to people in their pain.

Sermon ideas

(Optional activity: give out two pipe cleaners to each person. As you are talking through the first point, encourage people to use one pipe cleaner to manipulate as they like. As you continue with the second point, encourage people to use the second pipe cleaner. After the story illustration people can be invited to bring their pipe cleaners to a table or altar and connect their creation to another person's pipe cleaner creation. This could lead on to a time of prayer.)

Pain as a connector to your body

Humans have a body that is very perceptive of individual needs. The tensions and symptoms experienced by the body are messages to note and take required action.

Pain can be a sign that something is not right in the body. Sometimes these signs are ignored, so further pain can ensue. Pain can be a connector to looking after ourselves in a better way, taking time to observe and listen to the body, making it easier to stay on the path of health.

When having to cope with pain, emotions such as fear can be induced. Some people try and keep the pain subdued with constant medication, others let the pain rule their lives. God offers a way through the fear, inviting us to acknowledge the pain and to sit with it in his presence. He does not always offer a way out of our pain but uses it to develop faith and to sculpt us into the person he has made us to be.

Pain as a connector to God and eternal life

God sent his Son Jesus to show how he identifies with humanity by fully experiencing its mental, emotional and physical pain. Isaiah chapter 53 forecasts the abuse suffered by Jesus: 'He was despised and rejected by others; a man of suffering and acquainted with infirmity . . . we accounted him stricken, struck down by God, and afflicted.' The passage goes on to say what Jesus' sufferings did for us: 'he was wounded for our transgressions, crushed for our iniquities; upon him was the punishment that made us whole, and by his bruises we are healed' (Isaiah 53:3-5). The letter to the Hebrews reiterates that Christ faithfully and unflinchingly suffered, but he understood the violation and, consequently, modelled the hope that there is a God who cares deeply about the suffering, the injustice and the pain. He is one who empathises with our sufferings (Hebrews 2:17, 18).

Pain connects us to the suffering Christ. Peter encourages us to rejoice in this fact which will help make us more aware of God's glory being revealed. Pain can be used to focus on Christ, scattering what is not essential in our feelings.

Paul describes this suffering time as one of waiting – the pain being part of the tension that is carried within as we cope with life on this earth, whilst hoping for the promise of the advent of Christ. He compares this to the whole of creation that is groaning as in the pains of childbirth (Romans 8:22-25). Paul goes on to say that as we get tired in our waiting, the Holy Spirit is there to guide us and help us to express ourselves – especially through our prayers.

Pain as a connector to others

Paul associated with his pain and found that not only did it connect him to Christ but it also allowed him to minister more fully to others. The consolation he received through his afflictions he was able to pass on to others. 'He helps us in all our troubles, so that we are able to help others who have all kinds of troubles, using the same help that we ourselves have received from God (2 Corinthians 1:4, Good News Bible).

Pain can help us to be more aware of the suffering in the world and to have empathy for people we meet who are in pain.

Story

Mother Teresa had great mental and emotional pain over God's silence about suffering. She did not reject God; the pain became part of her. She was once given wise advice from a spiritual counsellor that helped her with this pain. He noted that there is no remedy for the darkness of suffering, so she should not take on that responsibility. Also Jesus had to suffer immense pain on the cross – he experienced the agony of separation from God. From this pain humankind was restored and people made whole. By holding onto God in the midst of darkness Mother Teresa could connect to the suffering Christ and also restore and heal.[31] She made her pain a bridge into the pain of others. In one of her letters she wrote, 'I have begun to love my darkness for I believe now that it is a part, a very small part, of Jesus' darkness and pain on earth.'[32]

Thought to take away

In Revelation 21:4 there is a promise that with the advent of Christ pain itself will be banished, for in that time God 'will wipe every tear from their eyes. Death will be no more; mourning and crying and pain will be no more'.

---

31. John Ortberg, *Faith and Doubt*, Zondervan, 2004. p.106.
32. http://www.motherteresa.org/13_anni/Reactionsandcomments.html.

Permissiveness

Alison Moore

Then they sent to him some Pharisees and some Herodians to trap him in what he said. And they came and said to him, 'Teacher, we know that you are sincere, and show deference to no one; for you do not regard people with partiality, but teach the way of God in accordance with truth. Is it lawful to pay taxes to the emperor, or not? Should we pay them, or should we not?' But knowing their hypocrisy, he said to them, 'Why are you putting me to the test? Bring me a denarius and let me see it.' And they brought one. Then he said to them, 'Whose head is this, and whose title?' They answered, 'The emperor's.' Jesus said to them, 'Give to the emperor the things that are the emperor's, and to God the things that are God's.' And they were utterly amazed at him.

Mark 12:13-17

Background information

If you ask someone what 'permissiveness' means their answer will probably give away their age. Anyone who remembers the 1960s is likely to associate the word with the 'permissive society', which in turn is associated with sexual permissiveness. The opening of Philip Larkin's 1967 poem 'Annus Mirabilis' neatly makes the point: 'Sexual intercourse began / in nineteen sixty-three.' Anyone younger – if they've thought about it at all – may see it as belonging to the history books, or perhaps referring to parenting styles. 'Permissiveness' is a term that raises eyebrows, implying attitudes or behaviour that are lax, not properly under control, and as such morally dubious. The particular aspect of the 1960s' 'permissive society' that troubled Christians and others was the way that sexual behaviour was separated from morality. And perhaps that explains why there is less interest in the term today, when in western society, at least, this separation is seen as uncontroversial. In theory at least, sexual behaviour is seen as morally neutral. Larkin's poem already critiques this in his ironic lines describing how after the sexual revolution, 'Everyone felt the same,/and every life became . . . /a quite unlosable game.'

However, sexual permissiveness was but a part of a much bigger issue about the individual and authority. The advocates of permissiveness in the 1960s were challenging the accepted authority bases of the day. 'Why should I conform to outmoded habits and institutions?' 'Why should sex be confined to marriage?' 'Why should I fight in a war I don't believe in?' The underlying question is, 'What right have you to tell me how to behave?', with its assumption that I don't need anyone's permission but my own.

Sermon ideas

'Render to Caesar what is Caesar's.' In its old-fashioned format, this phrase has entered common speech, as advice to respect the relevant authorities, whether we like it or not. But the second part of the saying is 'pay to God what is God's'. What did Jesus mean by this? He seems to be saying that there are areas of our life where we must respect God's way and God's demands.

Here we face the big question of how we make choices about how to behave, what authority we base this on. Christians would agree that our ultimate authority is from God, and that we base our behaviour on that. Of course, our understanding of what that actually means is where we differ. In our postmodern western world, the underlying premise of permissiveness has become uncontroversial and the rights and opinions of the individual are valued. Christians share this view. However, we know that this is not enough, and we cannot base our choices and behaviour just on our own individual opinion. Christians also believe that humans are made to live in community, which means institutions and organisations. Finding the balance between respecting the organisation and valuing the individual can be tricky. What belongs to 'Caesar' and what to God? There is undoubtedly a place for Christians to challenge the inward-looking attitudes of their churches if the organisation stops respecting the individual. In this sense Christians will always need to be open to being 'permissive', and to listen to the prophetic voice that follows a deeper authority, and critiques what the organisation is doing.

Story

Children's stories and folk stories often describe the frustrated younger sibling leaving home to find a better life. They choose the permissive pathway, rejecting or being rejected by their oppressive home life. The parable of the prodigal son has the same theme: the younger brother chooses the way of permissiveness, finds its limitations and returns to the home he now values. He is a changed and wiser person. The older brother who never risked the permissive path doesn't appreciate the values of what that home offers him.

Thought to take away

Where is the authoritative voice we recognise? How can we tell if it is God's or Caesar's? We respect individuals and organisations; we understand that permissiveness is sometimes from God, and if we are being asked to behave in a way that is contrary to Christian gospel, we may need the courage to speak out and do it differently.

Persecution

Chris Morley

Then one of the elders addressed me saying, 'Who are these, robed in white, and where have they come from?' I said to him, 'Sir, you are the one that knows.' Then he said to me, 'These are they who have come out of the great ordeal; they have washed their robes and made them white in the blood of the Lamb. For this reason they are before the throne of God and worship him day and night within his temple; and the one who is seated on the throne will shelter them. They will hunger no more, and thirst no more; the sun will not strike them, nor any scorching heat; for the Lamb at the centre of the throne will be their shepherd, and he will guide them to springs of the water of life, and God will wipe away every tear from their eyes.'

Revelation 7:13-17

Background information

Persecution is systematic mistreatment of an individual or group because of their religion, ethnicity, sexuality, or their political or social views. It can involve violence, harassment, imprisonment, expulsion from homes and homeland, even genocide.

On 10 December 1948, the United Nations General Assembly promulgated The Universal Declaration of Human Rights. This declared, among many other basic rights, that no one should be subjected to degrading treatment, arbitrary imprisonment or to attacks upon their honour and reputation. Everyone, it proclaimed, is entitled to freedom of thought, conscience and religion and the right to asylum if persecuted.

Persecution continues today and organisations like Amnesty International, the International Rehabilitation Council for Torture Victims (an umbrella organisation for 140 nationally based groups) and the International Criminal Court work to eliminate it. Many are persecuted for their opposition to the regime currently in power in their country. It's estimated that up to a million Christians face persecution, most of them in Muslim dominated countries.

Persecution can also be less systematic and without obvious cause as, for example, when bullying takes place in schools, churches, families, the workplace, and local communities.

Sermon ideas

In New Testament times, Christians suffered at the hands of both the Jewish and Roman authorities. High standards were demanded of those who were persecuted. They were not to be intimidated, and were always to be ready to give an account of what they stood for (1 Peter 3:14, 15).

Persecution of Christians continues today. Sometimes this is because of their work for human rights – severe violence against Christians in Central and South America in recent years is a good example – and not just because their religion isn't the predominant one. Some would say that when the Church is truly being itself, it is likely to attract persecution. But people without religious motivation also challenge abuse of power and are persecuted for their courage.

Jesus said that the persecuted will be blessed (Matthew 5:11, 12). He pointed to a reward in heaven and the passage quoted above offers similar recompense. Perhaps we can assume that such a reward is available to all who suffer persecution in the cause of justice, whether believers or not. Certainly many would doubt that there is any reward on earth. Very occasionally courage under persecution leads to change, as with black people in South Africa and the USA, but most of those persecuted feel unnoticed and powerless. Yet the contribution to our common humanity of those who bear it bravely is considerable.

Christian tradition points to Jesus as a model for dealing with persecution. In praying that his persecutors might be forgiven (Luke 23:34), he follows his own teaching (Matthew 5:44). Sadly this is often not what happens. Christianity having grown through, and partly because of persecution ('the blood of martyrs is the seed of the church' – Tertullian), has itself persecuted 'heretics' and people of other faiths. The Crusades, the Inquisition and countless religious wars are prominent historical examples but intolerance, if not actual persecution, is still occasionally a feature of the Church's and Christians' behaviour.

Our challenge, while supporting those being persecuted for their faith or struggle for justice, is to make sure fear of persecution isn't stopping us from being true to the gospel we stand for.

Story

Sadly there's an example of persecution in virtually every day's newspaper and current stories will be most effective. *Amnesty International's* website gives details of their current campaigns and some success stories. The newsletter of *Action for Christians against Torture* [acat(uk)], available on their website, gives details of people currently detained and invites prayers. The newsletter on the *Open Doors* website tells of Christians currently experiencing persecution. The website of the *International Criminal Court* details their current and previous investigations.

Thought to take away

Let us not forget: we are a pilgrim church, subject to misunderstanding, to persecution, but a church that walks serene, because it bears the force of love.

Oscar Romero, Archbishop of El Salvador, assassinated by government militia in 1980, having consistently spoken out in support of the hundreds of Christians and local parishes who had been threatened, arrested, tortured or murdered, for their support of the poor.

First they came for the communists
and I didn't speak out because I wasn't a communist.
Then they came for the trade unionists,
and I didn't speak out because I wasn't a trade unionist.
Then they came for the Jews,
and I didn't speak out because I wasn't a Jew.
Then they came for me
and there was no one left to speak out for me.

Pastor Martin Niemoller (1892-1984), referring to the inactivity of German intellectuals following the Nazi rise to power and the purging of their chosen targets, group after group.

Power

Joy Tetley

Christ the power of God and the wisdom of God.

1 Corinthians 1:24

Background information

The phenomenon of power is built in to the experience of life, whether that be in human terms or through the power of nature. It is multi-faceted in character, having many synonyms and forms of expression. A glance at any dictionary definition quickly brings home the range of senses and applications inherent in this one word 'power'. Power can be positive or negative in its outworking. It can be used and abused. It can be a force for good or ill. It can be controlled or uncontrolled (not least in nature). Similarly, it can both control and set free, destroy and build up. So much depends on how it is applied and experienced.

In the Bible and rabbinic tradition, 'power' is often a synonym for God (for example in Mark 14:62). For the believer, therefore, it is God who defines the true nature of power. God is its ultimate author, essence and epitome. Thus all earthly understanding of power needs to be tested against that of God. God's power is eternal. It is ever creative, self-giving, life-giving and redemptive. It is the power of pure love.

Sermon ideas

'Power tends to corrupt, and absolute power corrupts absolutely.'[33] So, famously, asserted Lord Acton, back in the nineteenth century. We do not have to look too hard to see the evident vindication of his claim. The marriage of power and corruption is all too prevalent. At any given time, examples abound. But we do, perhaps, need to look more deeply and ask some searching questions. Is power *always* a corrupting force? Can it not be a force for good? Power takes many shapes and is exercised in many and various ways. Can we think of examples from the world at large, or from our own experience, where power has been *empowering*, in the best sense of that word?

There can be no more 'absolute' power than that appertaining to God. What are we to make of that? Surely Lord Acton's pessimistic assessment cannot apply to God, can it? As in biblical times, we also often describe God as 'almighty' – the 'God of power and might'. Many of our prayers begin with the words, 'Almighty God . . . ' What do we mean by this? How does God exercise divine power? Is such power *really* all-powerful? If so, why are we not more aware of it in situations of suffering and horror? If God is God, then God's power must be the defining truth of all power. But it faces us with so many questions. How are we to understand these things?

It is in Christ, 'the power of God and the wisdom of God' (1 Corinthians 1:24), that the definition of godly power is most fully expressed and perceived. We need to look to Jesus to see more clearly. In Christ, we see that God's power is exercised, not in self-interest, not for self-aggrandisement, not to achieve control, but always in the interests of others, to enable flourishing, the realisation of potential and the bringing of all things to their intended and longed-for fulfilment (see Ephesians 1:9, 10; Colossians 1:15-20). As Jesus makes clear, it is exercised, not least, on behalf of the oppressed, the marginalised, the sick and the vulnerable.

This is highlighted for us in the Greek word for power most often used in the New Testament. It is *dunamis*, from which we derive the word 'dynamite'. This is explosive power which most certainly makes a difference. But in God's hands, that difference is entirely positive, as we see, for example, from the description of Jesus' miracles in the Synoptic Gospels (Matthew, Mark and Luke) as *dunameis*, acts of power (for example Mark 6:2, 5). This divine dynamism is most focally displayed in God's raising of Jesus from the dead (for example 1 Corinthians 6:14; 2 Corinthians 13:4). It is also used creatively in bringing Jesus into the world. As the angel said to Mary at the Annunciation, 'the power *(dunamis)* of the Most High shall overshadow you' (Luke 1:35). So we encounter the great paradox of the incarnation – God comes among us in human form, voluntarily setting aside divine omnipotence that we might know more fully the saving power of divine love (Philippians 2:5-11).

This is most starkly exposed, and is at its most challenging, in the power of God as expressed in Christ crucified. As Paul so acutely observed in his correspondence with the Corinthians, what presents in human terms as the epitome of shame and weakness is, in truth, divine power in action, that which brings us salvation in the fullest sense of that word (see 1 Corinthians 1:18-25). For here, truly, without a trace of corruption, is the absolute power of pure love, the love of God which goes to hell and back to offer us that life which is life indeed. The power of *this* love makes all the difference in the world.

Story

On 8 May 1373, in the city of Norwich, a young woman lay dying. The priest had been called. He held a crucifix before her eyes, urging her to gaze upon it. As she did so, hovering between life and death, she saw, not a man-made object, but a vision of God focused on Christ crucified. What that vision revealed to her was the surpassing power of God's love. Even while still *in extremis*, she realised that this was, quite literally, the crux of the matter, the meaning behind all things.

Against all expectations, she recovered. She spent the rest of her long life pondering and praying about what she had seen of God during that life-threatening crisis. At some point, she became an anchoress, associated with St Julian's Church in Norwich, devoting her life to prayer and the giving of counsel to others. She also produced a book about her visionary insights, the first known book by a woman in English, a book we can still read with much benefit today under the title, *The Revelations (or Showings) of God's Love*. Because of the church she lived next to, she became known as Julian of Norwich, but we do not know her real name. The following quotation is typical of her perception of the power of God's love:

'For I saw and knew that his marvellous and utter goodness brings our powers up to their full strength. At the same time, I saw that he is at work unceasingly in every conceivable thing, and that it is all done so well, so wisely and so powerfully that it is far greater than anything we can imagine, guess, or think.'

The Revelations of Divine Love,
translated by Clifton Wolters, (Penguin Classics, 1966),
chapter 45; cf. Romans 8:28, 39; Ephesians 3:20, 21

Thought to take away

The power of love is infinitely greater than the love of power.

33. Lord Acton, Letter to Bishop Mandell Creighton, 3 April 1887 – in Louise Creighton, *Life and Letters of Mandell Creighton*, Longmans, 1904, Vol.1, chap.13.

Prejudice

Joy Tetley

Just then his disciples came. They were astonished that he was speaking with a woman, but no one said, 'What do you want?' or 'Why are you speaking with her?'

John 4:27

Background information

Prejudice, it seems, is well nigh endemic in the human condition, both down the ages and around the world. As the word suggests, it involves making a judgement before properly considering the evidence. That pre-judgement then constitutes the basis for consequent attitudes and behaviours.

Prejudice can have many and various roots and can present in a multitude of forms. It is thus notoriously difficult to address. As Frederick the Great of Prussia put it in a letter to Voltaire back in the eighteenth century, 'Drive out prejudices through the door and they will return through the window.'[34] Samuel Johnson put it another way, 'Prejudice, not being founded on reason, cannot be removed by argument.'[35] (Though one might perhaps dare to hope that such an assessment might sometimes prove a little too pessimistic!) Not infrequently, prejudice is associated with familial, tribal, sectarian or national conditioning, passed down through the generations and often accompanied by passionate 'justifying' narratives. It can be targeted at individuals or categories of people – often, of course, at individuals *because* they belong to such categories. It frequently has to do with race, religion, gender and sexuality, perceived injustices and long-standing enmities. Profound and largely unexamined fear can often underlie prejudice, as can the desire to defend one's own perceived identity and interests. It can have devastating and destructive consequences. It can poison the soul of both pre-judger and pre-judged.

It is interesting that the word for prejudice is used only once in the New Testament (1 Timothy 5:21) and that in the fairly neutral sense of not showing partiality. However, the reality and character of prejudice are most certainly portrayed in the Scriptures – sometimes uncritically, as at Titus 1:12, 13, where a proverb describing Cretans as 'liars, vicious brutes and lazy gluttons' is approvingly quoted! More usually in the New Testament, the person, message and behaviour of Jesus challenge many forms of prejudice, emphatically affirming that the love, and therefore the mission of God are fully inclusive and all-embracing.

Sermon ideas

Prejudice is poisonous, and for all concerned. It is destructive of truth and love. It distorts vision, deadens the mind and hardens the heart. The exercise of prejudice often provokes attitudes and behaviours which are 'like-for-like', thus trapping the participants in a vicious circle. It can come from all manner of sources and have all manner of foci but its outcome is invariably negative. Typically, prejudice reduces persons to categories, caricatures and projected constructs, rather than the unique and complex individuals they actually are. Behind prejudice often lie fear and grievance, whether rooted in the past or the present (or, indeed, a potent combination of the two).

What can Jesus show us about this pernicious and pervasive phenomenon? Consistently, by his teaching and his behaviour, Jesus challenged the attitudes and assumptions of prejudice. His encounter at a Samaritan well with a Samaritan woman presents us with a telling example. We notice first that this episode was not the result of an orchestrated strategy, nor a planned 'statement'. It emerged out of Jesus' everyday life and behaviour. He lived out his message, even when there were few to witness it. Always and everywhere, he practised what he preached.

Returning from Judaea to Galilee, Jesus had to pass through Samaria. As the Evangelist indicates (John 4:9) Jews and Samaritans endeavoured not to associate with one another. Their attitude towards each other was rooted in their religious history. Many centuries before, the territory of Samaria had stood in the northern kingdom of Israel, itself a breakaway state from the kingdom of Judah. In the eighth century BC, this northern kingdom fell prey to the conquering Assyrians, who significantly depopulated the area of its existing inhabitants, whilst also introducing large numbers of people from elsewhere in their empire. The Samaritans thus became a mixed-race community. Though they shared much with their Jewish neighbours in terms of religious heritage and practice, they were regarded by those neighbours as practising an impure version of the faith. Such a conviction also meant that Samaritans as a whole were not looked upon kindly. They were a despised 'category'.

We can see, therefore, why the Samaritan woman was so surprised that Jesus asked her for a drink (and that would have meant his using of a Samaritan drinking vessel – unthinkable for an observant Jew). Yet Jesus, setting aside considerations of race and religion, not only communicates with this woman but asks for her help in his need. In a real sense, she becomes a living version of the good Samaritan (see Luke 10:25-37 for that parable).

And she is a woman. Not only that, she is a woman of questionable morality, ostracised even by her own community. Why else would she be coming to the well alone in the heat of the day, unusual behaviour for a woman drawing water? Jesus, therefore, is not only setting aside racial and religious prejudice, he is also ignoring entrenched attitudes associated with gender and sexual behaviour. No wonder when his disciples returned 'they were astonished that he was speaking with a woman' (John 4:27). This was just not done, whether that woman be Jewish or Samaritan and particularly not on a one-to-one, 'unchaperoned' basis. Further, as Jesus correctly discerned, the woman he was conversing with and receiving ministry from, was (according to the views of the time) a sexual sinner. He should have given her the widest of berths.

But he did not. Indeed, he used this opportunity to delve beneath the prejudices to bring out some of the transforming realities of God's truth. So he talks of the living water he can offer, 'a spring of water gushing up to eternal life' (John 4:10-15). He speaks of true worship, 'neither on this mountain nor in Jerusalem' but, wherever located, 'in spirit and in truth' (John 4:20-24). And with this marginalised, Samaritan woman he shares the deepest truth of all. To her comment about the Messiah, he responds, 'I am he, the one who is speaking to you' (John 4:26). Prejudice is being challenged and breached, not by mere human agency but by the operation of God himself.

Story

In the latter part of the twentieth century, Diana, Princess of Wales, did much to challenge the prejudice and fear then associated with those suffering from

Aids. In particular, with her ungloved hands, she held the hands of those diagnosed with this condition. This simple, caring action spoke more powerfully than many well-intentioned words and exhortations.

Thought to take away

God's love is all-embracing and breaks down all barriers.

---

34. Letter to Voltaire, 19 March 1771, in *Frederick the Great – Complete Works* by Thomas Carlyle, Cambridge University Press, 1790, Vol.12.
35. Quoted in H. Ward and J. Wild, *The Lion Christian Quotation Collection*, 1997. p.149.

Pride

John Cox

When pride comes, then comes disgrace; but wisdom is with the humble.
Pride goes before destruction, and a haughty spirit before a fall.

Proverbs 11:2; 16:18

Background information

Pride can be both a good thing and a bad thing.

To have a sense of one's own identity and to feel that what one is and does is satisfactory gives rise to an appropriate and valuable sense of pride. It is in this sense associated with a sense of self-worth which is very important. There can be a similar sense of pride in those people or groups one belongs to or associates with. So one can have pride in a football team or colleagues at work or a family. Pride in a successful achievement, especially if it has earned the praise of others, can arouse a sense of exhilaration.

To have a falsely high opinion of oneself and one's abilities and to parade that in the face of others is to exhibit an inappropriate pride which in religious terms is seen as a vice and is condemned in the Jewish and Christian traditions, as well as in other religions.

It is similarly possible to have a good and bad sense of pride associated with ethnic origins. 'Asian Pride', i.e. pride among the people of Asia, developed in part as reaction against western colonialism but also out of an appreciation of historic cultures and civilisations. 'Black Pride' is largely found among American Africans and emerged from the humiliation of slavery and racism, and resulting in the development of a confident black identity. 'White Pride' has generally been associated with movements for white supremacy.

Sermon ideas

Pride we are told goes before a fall. And certainly that is one way of viewing the story in Genesis of Adam and Eve's disobedience to God's command regarding the fruit of the tree of the knowledge of good and evil. Out of pride, it is suggested, they thought they had the right to such knowledge – a knowledge God was reserving to himself. Their action is widely known as the Fall.

But pride can be more subtle than that. It can prevent the experience of something that would be enjoyable or beneficial for the person, but pride gets in the way. Such was the experience of Naaman, the commander of the King of Aram's army (2 Kings 5:1-19). Suffering from leprosy, he had been persuaded to go to Israel to seek out Elisha the prophet, whom it was said had the power to cure him of his disease. His pride was hurt when the prophet didn't even bother to go out to meet this great man, but sent a messenger to tell him to wash himself in the river Jordan seven times. Personal pride and pride in his country were both hurt for Naaman believed that the rivers of Damascus were greater than the Jordan. He was in danger of letting pride get in the way of his cure until his servant suggested he did what the prophet had told him. In the words of a Bob Dylan song: 'Swallow your pride; you will not die, it is not poison.' Naaman did so and was cured.

Boasting to others about how good or clever or successful we are, especially if by doing so we want to boost our own importance or belittle others, is itself a form of pride. Such pride has a false view of things. And the Bible has plenty to say about this kind of boasting. In writing to the Christians at Corinth, St Paul criticised those who were constantly comparing themselves with one another. 'We, however, will not boast beyond limits,' he tells them (2 Corinthians 10:13). 'Let the one who boasts,' he continues, 'boast in the Lord. For it is not those who commend themselves that are approved, but those whom the Lord commends' (verses 17, 18). In fact, acting as a fool, he does go on to boast. He boasts of his ancestry, of his ministry, his labours and his sufferings. What is different here is that he boasts not of his strengths but of his weaknesses. He boasts of those things that give God glory, writing of all those things he has done in order to build up those he writes to.

There is a proper pride in ourselves. Without it we lose all sense of our own worth. But the deepest sense of worth and therefore of pride is that which we have through our being 'in Christ' – through our association with him, our commitment to him, and his grace working in us.

Story

In the story of Oedipus, it is pride that brings about the killing of a father by his son. King Laius of Thebes had learnt from an oracle that he would be killed by his own son Oedipus, then only a baby. Ordered to get rid of the boy, a servant left him on a mountain to die. A shepherd rescues the infant Oedipus and takes him to Corinth where he is adopted by the king, Polybus. Learning through a rumour that he might not be King Polybus' own son, Oedipus makes enquiry of the Delphic oracle, who only tells him that he will kill his father and mate with his mother. Seeking to avoid this Oedipus leaves Corinth. On the road to Thebes he comes across his father Laius, neither realising each other's true identity. They quarrel about whose chariot has right of way. Out of pride neither would give way. Laius strikes out at the boy with his sceptre but Oedipus throws him out of his chariot and kills him, thus fulfilling the first part of the oracle.

Thought to take away

Forbid it, Lord, that I should boast,
save in the death of Christ, my God:
all the vain things that charm me most,
I sacrifice them to his blood.

Isaac Watts (1674-1748)

Prison

Ed Hone

For there is no distinction, since all have sinned and fall short of the glory of God; they are now justified by his grace as a gift, through the redemption that is in Christ Jesus, whom God put forward as a sacrifice of atonement by his blood, effective through faith.

Romans 3:22b-25a

Background information

Official statistics show the number of men and women in prison in Britain to be typically around the 90,000 mark[36], in institutions varying from top-security to open prisons. Of these, approximately 4,200 are women (4.8 per cent of the total prison population). Over 1,300 juveniles (15-17 years old) are incarcerated, along with over 7,800 18-20 year-olds.[37] These statistics for 2012 compare with a prison population of fewer than 20,000 in 1900.[38]

Sermon ideas

Prison is intended to perform a number of functions in society: to punish wrong-doers, remove dangerous people from general circulation, deter would-be offenders and re-offenders, and finally, to rehabilitate those imprisoned, so they may take their proper place back in society and have a good chance of avoiding committing further crime. Prison must be seen in the wider context of the entire justice system, which includes the work of Social Services, policing and law-enforcement, the court system, imprisonment whilst awaiting trial, the whole range of other justice measures open to the courts, and (usually) eventual release.

Both Peter and Paul were imprisoned in the course of their witness to Christ, as recounted in the Acts of the Apostles[39]; both had miraculous escapes, enabling them to continue their missionary activity. Paul's observation that 'all have sinned and fall short of the glory of God' (Romans 3:23) is a good starting point for a Christian approach to prison, chiming as it does with the words of Jesus to the accusing crowd in the episode of the woman taken in adultery, where he challenged anyone who had not sinned to cast the first stone, knowing that no one could. For Christians, prison is for the good of the prisoner, and the ordering and flourishing of society as a whole. It cannot be merely punishment or retribution, but is always with the hope that some good may come from a bad situation. Just as Paul says that we all fall short of God's glory, he adds that we are justified by the free gift of grace: afflicted with sin, and offered the remedy in Christ.

Our attitude towards prisoners is necessarily shaped by that of Jesus in his sermon on the last judgement, where the righteous are saved because they visited those in prison, and in doing so, visited Christ himself (Matthew 25:31-46). Whether we literally visit those in prison, or remember their welfare in other ways, will be dictated by our circumstances and abilities. This is where our prayer is important. We can pray for prisoners themselves; for their families and dependents; for an understanding of their wrongdoing and a desire to turn away from crime in future; for all who work in the prison system, that they do so in a humane and just manner; for those in prison who are especially vulnerable in any way; and for those preparing for release, those anxious about what life 'on the outside' will bring. It is also important that we pray for people in prison for crimes they did not commit, prisoners of conscience, and those, like Peter and Paul, sent to gaol for their faith. The Prison Reform Trust[40] is a charity which campaigns for the well-being of prisoners and their families, and can provide a useful starting point for Christians interested in prison-related issues.

Story

On 2 February 1990 Nelson Mandela, the most famous prisoner of modern times, was released after 27 years in gaol, 18 of which were spent in the notorious Robben Island prison. Imprisoned for his political activism against the apartheid South African government, Mandela symbolised the suffering of the oppressed people. Remarkably, he emerged from the harsh conditions of prison dedicated to peace, justice and reconciliation, and became a leader respected on the world stage. From prison, even *because* of prison, good had come.

Thought to take away

Paul notes that 'all have sinned'. A few verses later, he notes that 'the wages of sin is death' (Romans 6:23). In other words, no one deserves life. But the glorious saving words follow immediately on, 'but the free gift of God is eternal life in Christ Jesus our Lord'. God desires us all to live and to be free.

---

36. www.justice.gov.uk/statistics/prisons-and.../prison-population-figures. Accessed 30 July 2012.
37. Figures are for March 2012, and are taken from www.parliament.uk/briefing-papers/SN04334.pdf This document includes further statistics and analysis of the prison population, including trends. Some tables present Scottish statistics separately from those of England and Wales.
38. ibid.
39. Acts 12:1-19 and Acts 16:16-40 respectively.
40. http://www.prisonreformtrust.org.uk.

Promiscuity

Chris Morley

The body is meant not for fornication, but for the Lord, and the Lord for the body. And God raised the Lord and will also raise us by his power. Do you not know that your bodies are members of Christ? Should I therefore take the members of Christ and make them members of a prostitute? Never! Do you not know that whoever is united to a prostitute becomes one body with her? For it is said, 'The two will be one flesh.' But anyone united to the Lord becomes one spirit with him. Shun fornication! Every sin that a person commits is outside the body; but the fornicator sins against the body itself. Or do you not know that your body is a temple of the Holy Spirit within you, which you have from God and that you are not your own? For you were bought with a price; therefore glorify God in your body.

1 Corinthians 6:13b-20

Background information

For centuries casual or indiscriminate sexual relations were condemned by Church and society and for a very practical reason. Children born out of wedlock threatened the orderly passing down of property to legitimate heirs. Gradually such fears diminished, those guilty of promiscuity were no longer subject to severe public humiliation and sexual behaviour began to be seen much more as a private matter.

Words like slut, whore, and slapper are often used to describe promiscuous women. It's been assumed that they were the seducers, as Eve had tempted Adam, and they were usually the ones punished. Womanising men, however, have often been regarded more sympathetically but this extra leeway granted to men was challenged when some of those working for female emancipation advocated free love for women. The contraceptive pill also made promiscuity less of a risk for women.

An NHS survey in 2011 suggested that men are more promiscuous than women. They reported having 9.3 different partners on average, with a quarter of men boasting of more than 10 'conquests'. By contrast, women averaged 4.7 sexual partners in their lives, with a quarter having just one. Older generations reported having had many fewer partners.

Sermon ideas

In the Bible, sexual union is more than a purely physical activity. It unites the couple in a way that restores what Genesis sees as their original state, part of one flesh. They were separated in order that the woman might be a 'helper' to the man (Genesis 2:20-23) and so the assumed context for sexual relations is one of (mutual) help and support.

The body too is more than just a physical entity. We are made in the 'image of God' and the fact that 'the Word became flesh' (John 1:14) confirms the spiritual value of our physical humanity; unlike in some heresies where the human soul is seen as superior and separable from the rest, in the Judaeo-Christian tradition, our bodies represent our whole selves, mind and spirit as well as the purely physical. (The modern holistic approach to our human bodies makes the same assumption.) So what we do with our bodies in sexual intercourse impacts on and should express our emotional and spiritual selves and not simply be a response to physical urges.

So Christianity traditionally disapproves of promiscuity because it lacks a context of ongoing mutual care and the commitment of heart and mind as well as body. Normally such commitment would be expressed in marriage. But particularly with the advent of more effective birth control, sexual activity is often now seen as one of the ways a couple may express their enjoyment of each other or of exploring their longer term suitability for each other. In this sort of area Christians differ as to where appropriate love-making ends and promiscuity begins.

Standards are higher for believers than others: Paul invites believers to offer their whole body to God (Romans 12:1) and says that when they receive the Spirit, their bodies become the Holy Spirit's temple (1 Corinthians 6:19). So Christians will want to use their physical sexuality in a manner that reflects the love with which God's Spirit has filled them. Promiscuity for them is when that's not what's happening.

Story

Mozart's opera, *Don Giovanni*, describes the adventures of its highly promiscuous eponymous main character. William Hogarth's series of paintings, *The Rake's Progress*, depicts the sexual and other adventures of Tom Rakewell, the spendthrift son and heir of a rich merchant. In both these eighteenth-century artistic portrayals, the licentious heroes come to an appropriately unpleasant end.

In contemporary society, the opposite moral is often drawn. For example, the hugely popular *James Bond* films and the *Sex and the City* television series provide respectively male and female role models in which sexual activity is opportunist and casual. No adverse consequences for this behaviour appear in the storyline. Indeed the opposite is the case.

A 2008 study published in the *American Journal of Paediatrics* found that females aged 12-17 who watched *Sex and the City* and other shows with similar values were about twice as likely to get pregnant as those who did not, and teenage male viewers were more likely to impregnate someone.

Thought to take away

Increased sexual activity without commitment reflects a similar trend away from commitment in wider society. The number of marriages is down (by a third since 1981), care by children for their elderly parents is decreasing (Help the Aged says up to 300,000 elderly people in the UK can go a month without speaking to a family member or a neighbour), fewer people are committed to regular support for others. According to the Citizenship Survey for England in 2009-2010, the number of people informally volunteering at least once a month – for example to help elderly neighbours – fell to 29 per cent, down from 37 per cent in 2003.

Punishment

Tony Castle

Surely he took up our infirmities
and carried our sorrows,
yet we considered him stricken by God,
smitten by him, and afflicted.
But he was pierced for our transgressions,
he was crushed for our iniquities;
the punishment that brought us peace
was upon him.

Isaiah 53:4, 5a (New International Version)

Background information

According to the Christian press there was a huge increase in the number of Passion Plays performed around the country at Easter 2012; for example in London's Trafalgar Square, at the 'Soul by the Sea' Festival, Brighton, and in Preston. All were particularly well supported by young people. The plays portrayed an innocent man being punished by brutal capital punishment. As one of the criminals who hung beside Jesus on the cross said, 'We are punished justly, for we are getting what our deeds deserve. But this man has done nothing wrong' (Luke 23:41, NIV).

In modern times five purposes have been identified for punishment: incapacitation, deterrence, retribution, reform, reparation or restorative justice. The first three would fit Roman crucifixion. It could hardly be used to reform a wrongdoer!

Sermon ideas

Immediately after Christ's hideous death and puzzling resurrection his friends were totally bewildered. They had come to believe that Jesus was the promised Messiah, but that he should be shamefully executed was not in the script! Hiding away they read the Scriptures, prayed and, guided by the Holy Spirit, in Isaiah's Servant Songs they found the answer. Christ, the Suffering Servant, had taken on our infirmities, our sorrows; he was pierced for our transgressions. His punishment brought us peace. His crucifixion was not a deterrent or retribution but uniquely redemptive. Tens of thousands of people, over the centuries, have suffered the punishment of crucifixion, but only the one endured by the Man who was God was redemptive, only 'by his wounds were we healed'.

The reasons for punishment must, for Christ's friends and followers, never be revengeful or retaliatory and as parents, grandparents and, perhaps, teachers we should reflect on this. Those purposes of punishment are not consonant with the high ideals of our Saviour. Whatever our 'neighbour' does we are still called to love and care for him. The last two purposes, reform and restorative justice, show a care for the offender and reveal a desire for him, or her, to make amends and 'turn their life around'. This is as true of 'justice', or fairness, in the family as of criminal acts in the community. Wrongdoing demands some kind of punishment, whether this is two minutes on the 'naughty step', or a hundred hours of service to the community, or, if there is no other way, a custodial sentence.

In eighteenth century Britain there were 200 crimes for which you could be hanged, including pickpocket theft. Clearly that was wildly disproportionate and unjust. Christian teaching on love and mercy dictates that if there must be some form of punishment, it must always be proportionate to the wrongdoing.

Story

A young pupil, because of his unruly behaviour, was sent to the headteacher for punishment. The head left him waiting outside his room for a bit and then summoned him in. The boy looked nervously at the headteacher as he stood before his desk. 'You have never been to me before, have you, Simon?' the headteacher said. The pupil shook his head. 'I believe that you are a good boy and will not need to see me again,' the teacher continued. Opening an exercise book, he said, 'This is my punishment book where I record the names and actions of children who are sent to me for punishment. I am going to write your name, and what you did, in pencil because I believe that having to come and see me is punishment enough and in a few months' time I will be able to rub it out. You are not going to come and see me again, are you, Simon?' A relieved Simon never did!

Thought to take away

Our God, in Christ, has experienced the extreme of human punishment. He knows how vengeful and retaliatory it can be. In and through the same Christ he has taught that humans should strive to be loving, as he is loving, caring as he is caring. So punishment, when it is necessary, should always be proportionate and in keeping with this teaching and gospel values.

Rape

Jocelyn Bryan

It was now about noon, and darkness came over the whole land until three in the afternoon, while the sun's light failed, and the curtain of the temple was torn in two. Then Jesus, crying with a loud voice said 'Father, into your hands I commend my spirit.'

Luke 23:44-46a

Background information

Rape is a crime which is horrific and devastating. Most of the victims of rape are women[41] and many suffer long-term consequences from the trauma of this violation of their bodies and self-respect. It is not uncommon for victims to suffer from depression, drug or substance misuse, anxiety, post-traumatic stress disorder, self-harming and suicide. Although the statistics for 2010 show that 435,000 people suffered rape or sexual violence, it is believed that as many as nine in ten cases are not reported. The majority of rape cases happen in families and do not involve strangers, although many believe that sexual violence within a marriage or committed relationship cannot be rape. Victims are often vulnerable and powerless, living lives which sadly contain cycles of abuse. Fear, shame and social pressures frequently prevent victims from disclosing their perpetrators.

The convergence of violence, sex and power in an act of horrific violation evokes strong emotions and responses. Questions of morality, sexuality, blame and responsibility surround this emotive crime which occurs across all cultures and is often used as a weapon in war. Rape remains a contentious issue, but the physical and psychological cost to rape victims is devastating.

Sermon ideas

To preach on the subject of rape requires enormous sensitivity and discernment. Where do we go to find words of comfort and hope for the victims of rape? How does a preacher dare to speak into lives which have been so ruptured by violence, so traumatised and overwhelmed by the horror of violation, that many victims wish they had not survived? How do we speak into lives of such agony and perpetual torment recognising and not diminishing their ordeal, but at the same time not inadvertently re-traumatising victims? With these questions in mind, what I offer below is a way of bringing together the violent experience of the rape and the violence of Christ's crucifixion. But the crucifixion is not the end of the story and the resurrection offers us a powerful and transformative hope which demonstrates that violence and death need not consume us.

Rape leaves its victims ensnared by trauma, disorder, isolation, hopelessness, diminishment and powerlessness. They are held captive and oppressed by their now traumatised minds and bodies. Life contains nothing but fear and everything is tinged with guilt and self-blame. Shattered fragments or tangled threads are what remain of a life which before rape had purpose and a sense of self-worth. How might the gospel of grace enable a rape victim to gather up these fragments and construct a new beginning founded on hope? How might the gospel truth unravel the knotted threads and weave a cloth which can enfold one gently in love?

Rape is an outrageous sinful act of violence, oppression and injustice. The Christian understanding of sexual morality is completely breached by rape. For the victims of rape, sin has enveloped them and holds them hostage. They cry out for grace, freedom and healing.

In the crucifixion and resurrection of Jesus there is a convergence of violence and hope. The darkness, trauma and destruction of the cross was a place of violation and agony. At the cross Jesus was subjected to a violent death; the one who was innocent became a victim of sin. But the cross was also a place of silent agony, where pain was held. Can the cross become a place of connection and solidarity for the victims of violent trauma such as rape?[42]

Silence and fear permeate the passion narrative. The crucifixion is surrounded by the horror, guilt and helplessness of the disciples. The story of the lives of the disciples of Jesus lies in fragments, confused and lost, they hide away: silent and terrified, they have no sense of when or how their story will end. This experience of not finding an end to the story often characterises what happens in trauma. The horror is relived time and time again and there is no sense of hope. The victim is stuck in perpetual darkness. But, the shattering violence and agony of the cross does end and it ends in resurrection glory. This is the most powerful and hopeful ending of all.

The journey from the crucifixion to the glorious resurrection brings with it a new sense of meaning to the mess of what has been and once this new sense of meaning has been attained, then the reality of God's love and grace can be claimed. In cross and resurrection, the fragments are gathered and the open-ended narrative of trauma is drawn together by the hope offered to us in Jesus' resurrection. Silence, agony and fear are replaced by light and hope, which are woven into a new beginning that finds its meaning in God's love and grace. But the journey from the agony of the cross to the glory of the resurrection may be a long and painful one. The hopefulness of the resurrection and the new beginning it offers may take a considerable time to be realised for anyone who has experienced the traumatic violence and darkness of rape. Yet within the silence and the dark agony of life, the death and resurrection of Jesus always holds the promise of light. The suffering love of Christ can and does become a source of imagined hope in the silence and the mess. Our faith embraces this as the ultimate demonstration of God's love for each of us, whatever we experience in life. The long road to new meaning requires courage and faith, but the cross and resurrection hold the power to break open the closed system of darkness and become the source of life, giving meaning and hope for lives shattered by violence and pain.

Story

Julia survived, although there were moments when death seemed less than a moment away. The nightmare, the descent into a living hell continues to consume her. Terrified to go out, she feels isolated and tormented by the shame and disgust of her terrifying experience of rape. Ten years on, her life is still stuck in the silent world of agony which so many victims of rape inhabit. Even the constant, supportive love of her parents has not enabled her to restore any sense of normality to her life. But at least they believed her. Sometimes Julia wishes she had not survived the brutality and the violence. What was done to her she fears can never be healed, such violation has fractured her whole being. She can no longer love her body or herself.

Thought to take away

Many victims of rape remain silent. Rape is a violent, sexual crime which devastates lives. As Christians we believe in the life-giving good news of the gospel which proclaims freedom for the oppressed. Rape victims are held captive by what has been done to them and remain fearful and silent. How might we raise awareness of the horror of rape and provide safe support for victims, so that they can regain hope and trust in their future?

41. Only 8 per cent of rape victims are male: see The Stern Review Home Office Report 2010 http://www.homeoffice.gov.uk/publications/crime/call-end-violence-women-girls/government-stern-review. Accessed 23 July 2012.
42. See S. Jones, *Trauma and Grace: Theology in a ruptured world*, 2009 Westminster/John Knox Press for fuller discussion of the cross and trauma.

Reconciliation

Edgar Ruddock

Jesus came and stood among his disciples and said, 'Peace be with you.'

John 20:19

Background information

Much has been learned about the science of reconciliation in recent years. Whole academic disciplines, and economic systems have been built around a peace-making 'industry'. Much has been of real insight and value. But on its own, no system, no methodology, will provide the answer to the conditions of the human heart.

- The number of divorces in England and Wales in 2010 was 119,589, an increase of 4.9 per cent since 2009, when there were 113,949 divorces
- The divorce rate rose in 2010 to 11.1 divorcing people per thousand married population from 10.5 in 2009 (divorce in England and Wales 2010 statistics)
- 1 in 4 women will be a victim of domestic violence in their lifetime – many of these on a number of occasions. One incident of domestic violence is reported to the police every minute. On average, 2 women a week are killed by a current or former partner (source: Women's Aid)
- Much can be, and is, done to improve industrial relations in the UK and move beyond historical disputes based on power, class and wealth. For example, ACAS (the Advisory, Conciliation and Arbitration Service) states its aim as to improve organisations and working life through better employment relations.

Sermon ideas

In the Hebrew language the word for peace is *shalom* – often used today as a greeting. In its origin it is not an abstract word, like so many words in the English language. Rather, peace is an active not a passive word – it is as much about peacemaking and peace-keeping as it is about being 'at peace'.

Peace and justice have to go together for either to have validity. We are not called to work for peace at any price, but for peace that can last because true reconciliation has been allowed to happen.

Peace never comes free, or cheap. Peacemaking is always costly. Our theology of the atonement indicates that reconciliation between God and ourselves comes at a very personal cost – that borne by a peasant preacher on a rugged wooden cross. God's love is such that God takes the pain and cost of peacemaking into his own life.

In human terms this raises the question of who should take the first step towards reconciliation. Too often we hear the cry, 'I'll only apologise if you do first!' With God it is different, and so it needs to be for God's own people.

Story

During the 1980s a vicious and bloody war was raging in Mozambique between the supporters of the former colonial power, and the liberation movements. The Bishop of Maputo, then the youngest bishop in the Anglican Communion, frequently 'disappeared' from his home district. Saying nothing to anyone, he was travelling often alone and in great personal danger, in search of the leaders of those fighting from the bush. His aim was to build understanding, and discern whether and how negotiations for peace could be brought about.

When peace finally came to that troubled but beautiful land, much of the credit, unnoticed and unacknowledged, should have gone to this faithful soldier of the cause of peace, Bishop Dinis Sengulane.

Thought to take away

For Christians the road to reconciliation is not automatically easier just because of what we believe. Reconciliation, especially in our personal lives, will always be a challenge. But the call of faith is perhaps to find peace in making peace, not to see peace as a right, or something that just happens to us. Putting others before ourselves actually works – as Jesus says, 'Whoever finds his life will lose it, but whoever loses his life for my sake will find it' (Matthew 10:39, NIV).

Repentance

Helen Costigane

He is gracious and merciful, slow to anger, and abounding in steadfast love, and relents from punishing.

Joel 2:13

Background information

What do I do to make you love me?
What have I got to do to be heard?
What do I do when lightning strikes me?
What have I got to do . . .
When sorry seems to be the hardest word?[43]

'Repentance' in ordinary usage is defined as a person's regret, sorrow or contrition for an act or thought against another which is deemed unacceptable. Admitting our guilt, taking responsibility for wrongdoing, and making a commitment to becoming a better person might be hard enough. However, saying sorry to someone also opens us up to the possibility that our contrition may be rejected by the person who has been wounded by our actions. The risk that saying sorry and asking to be forgiven can fall on deaf ears, or fail to restore the relationship that has been ruptured, may inhibit us from taking that necessary step towards restoration and healing. 'Sorry', then, really can be the 'hardest word'.

Sermon ideas

This ordinary idea of repentance and restoration is very different from that expressed in the scriptures in terms of our relationship with God. Stories abound of the God who seeks out the 'lost sheep'[44] or rejoices over the repentant sinner.[45] In the scriptural understanding, the idea of repentance (*metanoia*) implies a change of heart, a recognition and confession of the wrong done and an acceptance of the challenge to respond to God's call (Psalm 51). Moreover, it implies an amendment of life so that the individual resolves to live rightly and avoid sin in future. There may also be an element of restitution involved or an attempt to reverse the harmful effects of the wrongdoing. However, repentance is not just one single act but an ongoing lifelong process of openness and responsiveness to God. Whether repentance is genuine or not is demonstrated by changes in a person's thoughts, words and deeds.

If we do have a barrier to asking or accepting God's forgiveness for something we have done, perhaps we need to consider what image we carry of God in the depths of our hearts. While we might give assent intellectually to the idea of God as merciful, loving and forgiving, is it the case that our real perception of God is one whose mercy and love have to be earned, who is deaf to our pleas and blind to our struggles? Let us pray that we come to know God, through prayer and reflection, not as a harsh judge but as a Father . . . and a Father who, when we take our first steps towards him, is already running to meet us.

Story

The gospel story of the prodigal son shows us a father who sets out to embrace the errant son even before the miscreant has a chance to manifest fully the confession of all his misdeeds (Luke 15:11-24). There is no question that he has to strive to be loved and to be heard. Having squandered his wealth, he begins a process of reflection on his life and what he has lost. This leads to an evaluation of his life, his journey home, and the beginning of an honest confession, when he is met halfway by the father who is moved with pity and tenderness. That he joins in the festive banquet that his father has prepared for him shows his receptivity to forgiveness. We can only assume that the young man did indeed amend his life in the light of his new awareness of himself as his father's beloved child, and his desire to respond to such love and acceptance.

Thought to take away

Who is God for me in terms of my thoughts of repentance, mercy and forgiveness? Is he the God of Joel, who is tender, compassionate and gracious? Is he the Father who runs to meet us?

---

43. 'Sorry Seems to Be the Hardest Word', © Copyright Elton John and Bernie Taupin (Rocket Records, 1976).
44. Luke 15:4-7.
45. Luke 15:8-10.

Responsibility

Paul Nicholson

But when he came to himself he said, 'How many of my father's hired hands have bread enough and to spare, but here I am dying of hunger! I will get up and go to my father, and I will say to him, 'Father, I have sinned against heaven and before you; I am no longer worthy to be called your son; treat me like one of your hired hands.' So he set off and went to his father. But while he was still far off, his father saw him and was filled with compassion; he ran and put his arms around him and kissed him. Then the son said to him, 'Father, I have sinned against heaven and before you; I am no longer worthy to be called your son.' But the father said to his slaves, 'Quickly, bring out a robe – the best one – and put it on him; put a ring on his finger and sandals on his feet. And get the fatted calf and kill it, and let us eat and celebrate; for this son of mine was dead and is alive again; he was lost and is found!'

Luke 15:17-24

Background information

Considered philosophically, the concept of responsibility is a complex one. It might for instance seem to depend on free-will; yet one group of thinkers, the so-called compatibilists, believe that people can be held responsible for their actions even if those actions can ultimately be shown to be determined. Furthermore, different categories of responsibility operate according to different criteria. Thus it is possible to be morally responsible for an act without being legally responsible for it. The limits of social responsibility are hotly debated, and some ethicists would want to extend the idea to include collective responsibility, so that I can be held to be (at least to some extent) accountable for the actions of a corporation or state to which I belong.

Sermon ideas

The turning point of Jesus' parable of the prodigal son comes when the young man comes to his senses, having reached his lowest point, and decides to take responsibility for his actions. He chooses to return to his father, admit his responsibility, and face the consequences. He is pictured making the long journey home, rehearsing a set speech as he goes, and when he finally meets his father he wastes no time in admitting his guilt.

If the response of the son at this point is admirable, the reaction of the father is intended to be surprising. It is as if he doesn't even hear the words that his son has so carefully prepared. Nor does he indulge in recriminations, nor deal out appropriate punishment. He is too focused on his desire to welcome the boy, and reincorporate him into the family, to spend time debating issues of responsibility. Note, however, that he doesn't exonerate his son either, downplaying or ignoring the gravity of his offence. It simply isn't shown to be an issue for him. And this, according to Jesus, is what our heavenly Father is like. He is wholly focused on love; first, his own love of his erring child, and, secondly, the love that he hopes in this way to draw out of the sinful child.

Does this mean that there is no point in acting responsibly, that we can behave in whatever way we choose, confident of the Father's tender forgiveness? Not at all. The taking of responsibility remains the turning point of this story. Without it, the son would have stayed in his pigpen, and never come back to receive his father's abundant forgiveness. Without an awareness of our own guilt, it is not that God will refuse to forgive us. Rather, we will not be conscious of that forgiveness, nor of the possibilities for a further and deeper relationship that it offers. It has been suggested that God gifted human beings with free will precisely so that they could respond to him in a free and loving way impossible to the rest of those parts of creation of which we are aware. It is in the exercise of that gift of free will that responsibility comes into play.

Story

The English singer-songwriter, Billy Bragg, in his song 'NPWA' (Elektra, 2000) – No Power Without Accountability – re-works the slogan of the American Revolution 'No taxation without representation', to suggest that both governments and major corporations, and those who run them, must take fuller responsibility for the ways in which they use the power their wealth and influence give them.

> The ballot box is no guarantee that we achieve democracy,
> our leaders claim their victory when only half the people have spoken.

> We have no job security in this global economy,
> our borders closed to refugees but our markets
> forced open.

A growing challenge in these first decades of the twenty-first century is to establish global mechanisms by which this responsible accountability can be enforced when it does not seem to be forthcoming voluntarily.

Thought to take away

Responsibility can easily seem like a heavy burden that I experience as having been laid upon me by other people or circumstances. Yet a sure sign of God at work in a situation is that there is a certain lightness of touch evident, even where the situation itself is difficult or threatening. Am I aware of responsibilities that I have that I bear lightly, or even joyfully, corresponding to Jesus' saying that 'my yoke is easy, and my burden light' (Matthew 11:30)?

Responsible behaviour

Rupert Bristow

Therefore, my beloved, be steadfast, immovable, always excelling in the work of the Lord, because you know that in the Lord your labour is not in vain.

1 Corinthians 15:58

Background information

There is a current emphasis on responsibilities to go hand in hand with the hard-won rights of people over many years – from political rights to equality issues, from the right to a name, a basic right under the United Nations charter, to freedom from poverty encapsulated in the 'Make Poverty History' campaign. So we have responsibilities to the environment, enshrined in international commitments (Kyoto) and intentions (Rio), responsibilities as (and to) taxpayers, to shareholders (perhaps) and, if we are politicians, to those who elected us. Interestingly, the few references to responsibility in the Bible are mainly about responsibility being denied for something bad happening, usually an untimely death (Joshua 2:19; Acts 20:26). Today, whether the pendulum has swung sufficiently, not enough or too much away from rights and towards responsibilities is a matter of opinion. Christians may like to ponder on the need to respect both rights and responsibilities in the light of Christ's teaching and example.

Sermon ideas

The French have a word, 'responsable,' for which there is an inadequate, long-winded English equivalent, 'the person responsible' or 'the responsible person'. By not having that word in English we consign the concept of responsibility to just that – a concept. It is depersonalising and avoids grasping the nettle of personal responsibility. Responsibility can be seen as an ideal virtue or a reason for resigning, if that responsibility is not discharged properly, but rarely do we describe ourselves or another as someone who is a 'responsable', who naturally accepts and works hard to meet their responsibilities gladly and responsibly.

Jesus has a heavy responsibility to fulfil the mission of God the Father to restore the covenant with the people of God, who have 'erred and strayed' a great deal for centuries. Part of that mission is to build up disciples in his Church to share the fruits of that responsibility met in his death and resurrection, leading St Paul to exhort the Corinthians to '. . . be steadfast, immovable, always excelling in the work of the Lord, *because* you know that in the Lord your labour is not in vain'. He goes further in Ephesians chapter one by spelling out 'the immeasurable greatness of his power for us who believe' (1:19) leading to that 'power at work within us . . . able to accomplish abundantly far more than all we can ask or imagine' (3:20).

'The responsibility is ours' (TRIO) is often used as a slogan for a church's stewardship campaign, usually in terms of money, though increasingly encompassing other gifts and talents too. Even this makes the concept a corporate matter rather than an individual matter, but at least it puts the onus where it should be: or does it? In a sense Paul is saying that we can only fulfil personal or congregational responsibility adequately if we organise and use the gifts that we have been given unconditionally by God, rather than squander them, like the prodigal son, or bury them without 'adding value', as in the Parable of the Talents. If we are to fully 'respond' (a word with similar roots as 'responsibility') to that abundance, freely given to us, then that response is the mainspring and the motivation to enable us to meet our responsibilities, both as Christians and as citizens, which are interwoven functions, not separate ones. And that means being 'steadfast' and 'immovable' in faith, which will then naturally lead us to look after neighbour, orphan and widow, feed the poor and clothe the naked, and even pay our taxes! There is an element of 'trust' or 'covenant' in all this too, just as the true 'responsable' (or person with responsibility) does not flaunt or misuse power, but seeks to enable and equip others to meet their responsibilities as well, which in the Church is a reason for majoring on mission alongside 'maintenance'.

Story

'Health and Safety' often gets a bad press. All those petty rules and regulations which seem to fall short of one key ingredient – common sense. So, in a well-publicised case that took place in 2007, two police community officers allegedly didn't try to rescue a boy at risk of drowning in a very cold lake, because they didn't have the required level of authority, responsibility or training to do so. In one sense they were acting responsibly and within their 'rights', but, in another sense, as fully responsible citizens ('responsables'), perhaps they should have considered what gifts and commitment and courage they had been given by God and just 'gone for it'. But of course even Peter ('The Rock') sank under the waves when he tried to emulate Jesus (Matthew 14:30). Being a Christian is not an easy task and we may all have our own stories of falling short in our greater responsibilities by hiding behind man-made ones.

Thought to take away

Let us examine our hearts. Is our Christian responsibility being discharged as well as our civic one? And how much do these overlap in our lives: do we see them as separate or each informing and supporting the other? To live an integrated life under God, we need 'to pray constantly' to be sure we can act responsibly when the test comes. We can indeed 'be steadfast, immovable, always excelling in the work of the Lord'.

Revenge

John Parr

Jesus said: 'So when you are offering your gift at the altar, if you remember that your brother or sister has something against you, leave your gift there before the altar and go; first be reconciled to your brother or sister, and then come and offer your gift.

'You have heard that it was said, "An eye for an eye and a tooth for a tooth." But I say to you, Do not resist an evildoer. But if anyone strikes you on the right cheek, turn the other also.

'You have heard that it was said, "You shall love your neighbour and hate your enemy." But I say to you, Love your enemies and pray for those who persecute you, so that you may be children of your Father in heaven; for he makes his sun rise on the evil and on the good, and sends rain on the righteous and on the unrighteous.'

Matthew 5:23, 24, 38, 39, 43-45

Background information

Revenge is the action people take when they retaliate after they have been offended or injured. It comes in many forms, from the football team that defeats its arch-rivals after losing their previous encounter, to the government that bombs the homes of known terrorist leaders. If we assume that there are limits to acceptable behaviour, and that wrongdoing should be punished, we may see a certain logic in revenge. When our desires are regulated by law, revenge may even accord with what we believe is 'natural' justice. At an appropriate level revenge can prevent dangerous behaviour from escalating, which is why the law of Moses sanctions the 'like for like' principle of 'life for life, eye for eye, tooth for tooth, hand for hand, foot for foot, burn for burn, wound for wound, stripe for stripe' (Exodus 21:23, 24). But at its worst, revenge breeds further violence. In words attributed to Mahatma Gandhi, 'An eye for an eye makes the whole world blind.'

Sermon ideas

In the Bible, revenge is written indelibly into the human story. Samson is an outstanding, though hardly unique, example (see Judges 14-16). The earlier stories of Cain and Abel, Noah, the Tower of Babel and the Exodus draw God into the world of revenge. The psalmists expect God to take revenge on Israel's enemies. Their God is so appalled by some human behaviour – especially that of his own covenant people at times – that he cannot help but retaliate. In the prophets, the 'day of the Lord' is the ultimate in divine vengeance that decisively clears the world of evil.

Those who believe in God's just vengeance use it to sanction their own actions. But the New Testament questions the easy acceptance of revenge. Jesus warns against letting the desire for revenge onto the holy ground of the Temple, where a pilgrim might be tempted to ask God to approve it. Instead worshippers are to make peace initiatives before arrival (Matthew 5:23, 24). Turning the other cheek rather than gouging out on eye breaks vicious cycles of violence (Matthew 5:39). Love for enemies does not mean that it is wrong to have enemies, only that revenge is out of the question (Matthew 5:43, 44). In the same vein, Paul encourages prayer for enemies and positive action that overcomes evil with good – the very opposite of revenge (Romans 12:14-21). The language of God's just vengeance remains (Romans 12:19; cf. Deuteronomy 32:35), only now it serves to limit rather than sanction imitative human behaviour.

When relationships break down, the desire for revenge soon turns toxic. An estranged couple may punish one another through their children – denying access, influencing their opinions, besmirching the other's character in front of them. Social media can be used to undermine the reputation of a colleague or school or workplace that has failed to live up to expectations. Actions like these only highlight the importance of finding more creative ways to resolve conflict.

Story

On 27 June 2012 Queen Elizabeth II shook hands with Martin McGuinness in Belfast. She is the head of the armed forces against whom the Irish Republican Army under his command once fought. Her cousin, Lord Louis Mountbatten, was one of the victims of the violence in Northern Ireland, when he was assassinated by the IRA in 1979. For the Queen and Martin McGuinness to shake hands so publicly, after an earlier private meeting, took some doing. They both had their critics and their demons to face. No one knows how far this was an act of forgiveness and reconciliation. But their willingness to distance themselves from the desire for revenge was a step forward in the Northern Ireland peace process.

Thought to take away

In today's world, the destructive capacity of revenge is increasingly wide-ranging, costly and threatening. At the push of a button, verbal and military missiles are released into cyberspace and airspace to work their mischief. Some religious teachings only exacerbate conflict, while others suggest more hopeful ways of dealing with the desire for revenge. Karen Armstrong encourages believers of all kinds to uncover the compassionate strands in their traditions, to 'provide an important counter-narrative in our discordant world'[46]

46. Karen Armstrong, *The Bible. The Biography*, London: Atlantic Books, 2007. p.229.

Risk

Paul Cox

Command those who are rich in this present world not to be arrogant nor to put their hope in wealth, which is so uncertain [risky], but to put their hope in God, who richly provides us with everything for our enjoyment.

1 Timothy 6:16, 17 (New International Version)

Background information

The Bible does not have many texts including the word 'risk' (about nine in all) but look up Wikipedia and there are over one billion possible sites to visit. We are living in a culture that wishes to reduce risks and risk taking. The Health and Safety Executive works hard to achieve risk-free (or should that be risk-reduced?) environments. The death rate has been greatly reduced in homes and places of work, such as farms (the most dangerous workplace, with deaths at eight per 100,000 workers)[47], in mines and in factories. That is all to the good, but some would say that too much health and safety legislation produces a 'nanny state' whereby people do not take responsibility for their own safety.

It is easy to have disproportionate ideas about risks. In a radio report it was stated that the risk of injury to children by falling out of bed was eight times greater than for tree-climbing children falling from trees! Too much protection from risk means that we become less aware of risks that inevitably occur, for we live in that kind of world. We may not even be properly aware of the nature of injury, about one third of people going to accident and emergency hospital departments did not need treatment.[48]

Sermon ideas

Jesus did not keep from those who would follow him the risks and dangers involved. 'Then he called the crowd along with his disciples and said, "Whoever wants to be my disciple must deny themselves and take up their cross and follow me"' (Mark 8:34, NIV). Not the most attractive invitation to be offered! He was just as realistic in telling his disciples the conditions to be faced in the mission field. 'I am sending you out like sheep among wolves. Therefore be as shrewd as snakes and as innocent as doves. Be on your guard; you will be handed over to the local councils and be flogged in the synagogues' (Matthew 10:16, 17, NIV).

To be told of the risks prepares us to both look out for them and to consider how we may deal with them. Risk taking may involve us in making choices. Being free to choose is a gift we all have within the loving relationship with God. To allow us such freedom is the greatest risk God allowed within his creative act. It had to be there if God was to create us to and for love. The account of the Fall tries to show how through a particular choice made, humanity is prone to make bad choices which lead to sin. To cancel out the eternal consequences of sin, God acted out of love. That is the Good News of the Incarnation, crucifixion and resurrection of Jesus.

Life is not, and never can be without risk. To venture into the unknown is always risky but the results of such venturing can mean that great discoveries have been made, great inventions developed and, most importantly, the human spirit has grown in wonder and awe. Risk taking is not to be legislated out of existence but should be celebrated. We develop and mature by how we deal with risk; not by denying it, nor by trying to remove it beyond our ability to make free choices. We may need help to recognise risks and how to deal with them in our secular life.

Although the risks of being Christ's disciple are not hidden, we are not without support and help. 'To deny oneself' means that we should place our trust in God. That leads to our acceptance that we cannot be completely in control; we acknowledge our vulnerability and place ourselves into God's care. That does not mean everything is then without risk. But it does mean that the final consequences are within God's purpose. It is with such a trust and acceptance of what being a disciple of Christ means that many people over the centuries have been faithful disciples and have even been martyrs. Belief in eternal life takes away the fear of death, and of facing risks in the service of Christ.

Story

Anxiety about making a mistake involves us trying to avoid risk. P. Fontaine tells the story of his college days. 'In my unforgettable college days, a boy who played next to me in the orchestra never made a mistake. But one day this lad ceased to be a member of the orchestra, and the professor told us why the boy never made a mistake. He did not play loud enough for anyone to hear him. It is human to err. Any man who is playing his God-given part in life may make a mistake, may do some wrong, he may be a victim of circumstances. The important thing is not the mistake he makes, but his reaction to that mistake and the circumstances surrounding it.'[49]

Thought to take away

It might be worth noting that the Chinese word for 'crisis' is spelt with two ideograms. One means 'risk' and the other 'opportunity'. In our discipleship we have the Bible, the example of Jesus and the Holy Spirit to help us meet risks and to overcome them and even to use them as an opportunity to serve our Lord.

---

47. Health and Safety Executive report 2010/11.
48. *Daily Mail*, 19 January 2011.
49. Quoted in *Complete Quotes and Anecdotes*, compiled by Tony Castle, Kevin Mayhew 2007.

Scandal

Clare Richards

Jesus said: I am the Way, the Truth, and the Life.

John 14:6 (Jerusalem Bible)

Background information

We seem to be bombarded today by the media with scandals. A scandal is an action regarded as morally or legally wrong, which outrages our sensibilities. Journalists, politicians and even the Church are now subject to close scrutiny, as we witness some of those we thought we could trust behaving in totally unacceptable ways, prompted by greed, power or sinful wrongdoing. It is not always the case that people try to hide their scandalous behaviour. The actions of some people cause scandal because they act in a way that goes against public approval. An older generation may be scandalised by the lifestyle of the younger one. 'We didn't behave like that in our day!' Jesus was seen to be a scandal by the Pharisees as he socialised with prostitutes and tax-gatherers.

Sermon ideas

We have been outraged in recent times by realising that some of those people in whom we put our trust have been hiding the truth behind their actions. Scandals in journalism, political life and within the Church have filled our newspapers. The origin of the word 'scandal' comes from the Greek 'skandalon' meaning a 'stumbling block'. In Middle English it was understood as 'discrediting religion by bad behaviour of a religious person.'[50] In other words, if we are really serious about following Christ, the Way, the Truth and the Life, then we should realise that our faults and sinfulness can be a stumbling block, a scandal to others.

Christ calls us to live by the Truth. In the fifth century, St Augustine said 'Nothing conquers except truth: the victory of truth is love.'[51] Christ's love for us led him to crucifixion. Paul was the first to describe the 'Scandal of the Cross'. The cross is a scene of failure, and disgrace. Paul told the Corinthians: 'Here we are preaching a crucified Christ: to the Jews an obstacle that they cannot get over, to the pagans madness' (1 Corinthians 1:23, Jerusalem Bible).

The scandals in journalism may make us feel that we can never have faith in what we read. But we can have faith in the first Christian journalists, the four evangelists, who recognised Christ as the Truth. They point the way for us to follow him by putting the needs of others before our own. Luke describes the 'manifesto' Jesus gave as he began his public life. In the Nazareth synagogue, using the words of Isaiah, he said he was sent to give good news to the poor, to prisoners, to the blind and the downtrodden. Matthew tells us that Jesus identifies himself with the most disadvantaged people. 'For I was hungry and you gave me food. I was a stranger and you made me welcome' (Matthew 25:35, Jerusalem Bible). The evangelist is telling us that loving compassion for others is the only criterion on which we will be judged.

Story

It is good news that many Christians have followed Christ by seeing him in others. Eglantine Jebb was born into a devout Anglican Victorian family in 1876. One of the first women students at Oxford University, she delighted in her studies and in dancing, hockey and rowing. As a teacher she visited the homes of her pupils and, horrified at their poverty, yearned to serve Christ in the poor at whatever cost to herself. Choosing to help children in the greatest need she went out to Greece to help refugees escaping the Balkan War. It resulted in her founding 'Save the Children Fund' and travelling to the Balkans, Africa, India, Russia and China. She was to cause a scandal back at home. A good one! She was arrested and prosecuted in London for handing out leaflets showing starving babies. It was Pope Benedict XV who first came to her support. Today she is commemorated in the Anglican Church on 17 December.

Thought to take away

The evangelists report that Jesus tells us to love God with all our heart, and to love our neighbours as ourselves. Mark tells us that this means we will have to take up our cross (Mark 8:34). Are we prepared to be a scandal to others for his sake? John, writing years later, reminds us that Jesus also said: 'Do not let your hearts be troubled. Trust in God still, and trust in me', going on to say 'I am the Way, the Truth and the Life' (John 14:1, 6, Jerusalem Bible).

It may help us to really understand what Christ asks of us by taking time to read quietly John's deep reflection on our response to God's love. It is found in the Farewell Discourses, John 13:33 to the end of chapter 17.

50. Oxford Dictionary of English, 2006.
51. Quoted in *Quotes and Anecdotes for Preachers and Teachers*, Tony Castle, Kevin Mayhew, 1979. p.139.

Secularism

Ed Hone

So when the woman saw that the tree was good for food, and that it was a delight to the eyes, and that the tree was to be desired to make one wise, she took of its fruit and ate; and she also gave some to her husband, who was with her, and he ate.

Genesis 3:6

Background information

British society is becoming increasingly secular, and any overt expression of religious belief can potentially cause controversy, whether it be the wearing of a cross at work, a face veil in public, or beginning meetings with a prayer. Religion is more and more regarded as belonging to the private domain, personal rather than social, and certainly not appropriate for the civil sphere.

Sermon ideas

The eating of the forbidden fruit in Genesis is usually understood as being primarily about disobedience and its age-long consequences. But there is another layer of meaning relevant here: Adam and Eve, unable to control their desires, settled for something disastrously short of what God was offering them.

A common Christian approach to secularism advises that we should resist the siren calls of secular society, discipline our will and keep our desires under control, lest they lead us astray. There is wisdom in this advice, of course, but of itself it is not sufficient. C. S. Lewis captures the paradox of human desire, identifying what lies at the core of secularism:

Our Lord finds our desires not too strong, but too weak. We are half-hearted creatures, fooling about with drink and sex and ambition when infinite joy is offered us, like an ignorant child who wants to go on making mud pies in a slum because he cannot imagine what is meant by the offer of a holiday at the sea. We are far too easily pleased.'[52]

It is not our desires, then, that are the problem, but *what* we desire. Secularism is not necessarily the denial or rejection of God, but rather the substitution of God by something else. This substitution can be deliberate or accidental, conscious or unconscious; we can feel helpless in the face of it, or seek to counter it in the belief that we should and must.

Any number of things can be at the centre of a secular world view:

- consumer culture, where we believe acquisition makes us happy;
- an entirely scientific approach to life, where we believe that science has the answers to all human questions;
- political ideology, where human fulfilment is seen as achievable by the perfect political system;
- a philosophy of self-development, where we each pursue health of body, mind and spirit as the ultimate goals of life.

And this is where the seductive nature of secularism can be seen for what it is: any of the things we substitute for God may be good in themselves, but if we settle for them we're selling ourselves short. We are made for bigger and better: made for God; anything else ultimately won't do.

So where does this leave us? Let's return to the Genesis account of the Fall. If only Adam and Eve could have truly understood what God was offering them; if only they could have imagined the frustration and pain their exile from Paradise would cause them; if only they could have appreciated the privilege of their intimacy with God. So many 'if onlys'! Our best response to secularism is to ensure God is at the centre of our lives. To achieve this, we read the scriptures, reflecting on the ways of God; we ponder the teachings and life of Jesus; we seek to become imbued with the Spirit of the risen Christ; we pray, availing of the intimacy God offers us; we worship God, and are reminded of the salvation God promises to us; we love and serve our neighbour, modelling kingdom values that contrast with those of secular society, because they are from God. And when we're doing all this, we continue to engage with the world beyond the Church, the world which Jesus came to save.

Story

In his epic poem *Endymion*, John Keats writes, 'A thing of beauty is a joy for ever: Its loveliness increases; it will never pass into nothingness . . .' We Christians recognise the truth of this, knowing we will find eternity, true peace and ultimate beauty in God. We will not know true rest until we are fully in God.

Thought to take away

Jesus answered her, 'If you knew the gift of God, and who it is that is saying to you, 'Give me a drink', you would have asked him, and he would have given you living water' (John 4:10). We pray that we might understand more fully the gift of God, and share our faith with others.

52. C. S. Lewis, *The Weight of Glory and Other Addresses*, Collier: New York, 1980.

Slander

John Parr

The scribes who came down from Jerusalem said [of Jesus], 'He has Beelzebul, and by the ruler of the demons he casts out demons.' And he called them to him, and spoke to them in parables, 'How can Satan cast out Satan? If a kingdom is divided against itself, that kingdom cannot stand. And if a house is divided against itself, that house will not be able to stand. And if Satan has risen up against himself and is divided, he cannot stand, but his end has come. But no one can enter a strong man's house and plunder his property without first tying up the strong man; then indeed the house can be plundered.

'Truly I tell you, people will be forgiven for their sins and whatever blasphemies they utter; but whoever blasphemes against the Holy Spirit can never have forgiveness, but is guilty of an eternal sin' – for they had said, 'He has an unclean spirit.'

Mark 3:22-30

Background information

Slander is hostile speech that relies on falsehood to attack others. By calling into question a person's actions and motivation, it undermines self-esteem, reputation and social standing. Slander helps to create a climate of suspicion and cynicism, which ultimately rebounds on its source as well as its object. Given the power of slander, we can well understand the commandment to avoid false witness (Exodus 20:16) as part of a general concern for the kind of speech that promotes individual and social well-being.

Stigmatising language is a particular form of slander, because it invites its audience to think the worst of those whom it labels. In Jesus' day, people were stigmatised as 'sinners', 'demon-possessed', 'unclean' or 'Gentiles'. Today terms like 'mental', 'chav' and 'pervert' function in the same way. They are pieces of shorthand that evoke supposedly definitive stories about the people they refer to. There is something 'wrong' with such 'inadequate' and 'unsavoury' people, so that it is wise to keep them at a distance.

Sermon ideas

Jesus' attitude to slander is part of his concern to rehabilitate the reputations of marginalised people. We see this in the way he calls into question the presumed connection between particular kinds of sickness and 'sin'. Just because a man is disabled, this does not give anyone the right to think the worst of him or his family (John 9:2). By challenging such stigmatising slander, Jesus put himself in the recipients' place. So it is not surprising that he should also become an object of slander when his power is ascribed to the devil (Mark 3:22). Jesus rose above his enemies' regular recourse to slander. Rather than adopt their tactics, he exposed the absurdity of their attack (Mark 3:23-27), and his silence before his accusers is an object lesson in neutralising their power (Mark 14:61).

Slander spreads easily and quickly through gossip, with its careless talk and unsubstantiated rumours that hearers fail to check for themselves. Social media only amplify the problem by multiplying the potential audience and creating a permanent record of a victim's supposed character or misdemeanours. The website www.ceasefireproject.com has been created by Christians who have suffered as a result of internet slander. Rather than playing down contentious issues, Ceasefire encourages Christians to resolve their differences without recourse to slander.

Story

The Anglican priest, columnist and broadcaster Giles Fraser is no stranger to dispute, in the flesh or in print. What he writes about the dangers of blogging applies to slander more generally:

> On the internet, the other does not come with a face. The French philosopher and Talmudic scholar Emmanuel Levinas has based his ethical philosophy on the sense of responsibility for others that originates in the face-to-face encounter. Only by looking at someone's face does one properly appreciate his or her vulnerability – a vulnerability that cries out not to be harmed.
>
> The quick-fire argument on the internet has cut itself adrift from this sensitivity, and has become cruel. This is why too much time going through blogs and comments can be bad for your spiritual health.[53]

The more we distance ourselves from each other's vulnerability, the less likely we are to 'speak the truth in love'. This is the antithesis of slander, and it thrives wherever Christlike virtues flourish (Ephesians 4:15, 25-32).

Thought to take away

How might we avoid slander by 'speaking the truth in love'? It is not always possible to speak well of others, but when criticism is called for, these words suggest that it should be offered with respect, in an informed way that eschews stigmatising stereotypes. We avoid slander when our speech reflects virtuous attitudes and promotes healthy social relations in the Church and wider world.

53. *Church Times*, 29 April 2009.

Sterilisation

John Parr

I appeal to you therefore, brothers and sisters, by the mercies of God, to present your bodies as a living sacrifice, holy and acceptable to God, which is your spiritual worship. Do not be conformed to this world, but be transformed by the renewing of your minds, so that you may discern what is the will of God – what is good and acceptable and perfect.

Romans 12:1, 2

Background information

Sterilisation is a range of surgical procedures that make a woman or a man incapable of reproduction. These include closing the fallopian tubes (tubal ligation) and removing the uterus (hysterectomy) in women, and vasectomy in men. Some of these are carried out for medical reasons, while others are forms of contraception. Sterilisation is also used in gender reassignment (sex change). Most people who undergo voluntary sterilisation suffer no ill effects, and few regret their decision.

During the twentieth century compulsory sterilisation was used in several countries – including Canada, USA, Peru, India, China, Japan and Sweden – as a form of birth control, with the aim of preventing the spread of hereditary conditions and reducing the population of minorities. In Puerto Rico, a government-backed programme brought about the compulsory sterilisation of one third of the women by 1965. Where compulsory sterilisation is part of a widespread or systematic action by a government, the International Criminal Court regards it as a crime against humanity.

Sermon ideas

The Bible makes no direct reference to sterilisation. We might assume its writers would take a low view of voluntary sterilisation for contraceptive reasons, in view of their estimate of the importance of human reproduction (see Genesis 1:28). Men with crushed testicles may not have been sterilised, but they were nonetheless excluded from the worshipping community of Israel (Leviticus 21:20). Eunuchs – men who have been sterilised by castration – were employed as civil servants by foreign rulers (Esther 1:10; Acts 8:27), but not in Israel or Judah. Yet even they can hope to find a place in God's salvation (Isaiah 56:3-5). When Jesus referred to those 'who have made themselves eunuchs for the sake of the kingdom of heaven' (Matthew 19:12), he was more likely to have been speaking figuratively of voluntary celibacy as an example of the single-mindedness demanded by the coming of God's reign, rather than commending castration as a condition of discipleship.

The contemporary practice of sterilisation – for medical or other reasons – is an example of our ability to re-make human bodies in our own image. Where this happens without consent, it can be seen as a form of abuse. Where sterilisation is freely chosen as a means of contraception, it is interpreted by some Christians as an example of 'playing God' and by others as an act of faithful and responsible living.

Paul's injunction to 'present your bodies as a living sacrifice, holy and acceptable to God' (Romans 12:1), underlines the conviction found throughout his writings that experience of God's salvation is always embodied. 'Spiritual worship' extends beyond liturgical activity into sexual behaviour, eating and sharing food, dress codes and community relations. In the absence of direct guidance on issues of concern for contemporary Christians (and sterilisation is only one of these), the Bible can be understood as a series of communications from the past, where 'they do things differently'. Contemporary wisdom will be informed by its narratives of faithful living without being constrained by them. This involves asking whether we can envisage voluntary sterilisation as an example of the offering of our whole lives to God.

Story

Joe and Emma are in their early thirties and have three children. Before they had children, they felt that two would be enough. The third was a 'surprise', and they soon learned to welcome her. But they believe a fourth would be irresponsible. Emma has been taking the contraceptive pill for nearly 15 years, and does not relish the prospect of continuing until the menopause. They both want a form of contraception that is as near to 100 per cent reliable as possible. For Joe to have a vasectomy would be the simplest option. But they wonder about the 'what ifs'. Two couples in their circle of friends have recently split up. And eighteen months ago the 6-year-old son of Emma's sister died in a road accident. As well as discussing their concerns with Joe's GP, they decide to talk to their pastor, especially after discovering some challenging websites from the more conservative end of the Christian spectrum.

Thought to take away

As a lifestyle choice that allows worry-free contraception, the rightness of voluntary sterilisation may be called into question by the obvious risk factors faced by Joe and Emma. Many are prepared to act in good faith, live in hope and take the risk – or pay the price of further surgery should this become desirable or possible. Yet the moral issues surrounding voluntary sterilisation are not unique. They are an example of what we expect when we walk by 'faith' rather than 'sight' (2 Corinthians 5:7).

Superstition

John Cox

The spirit of the Egyptians within them will be
emptied out,
and I will confound their plans;
they will consult the idols and the spirits of the dead
and the ghosts and the familiar spirits;
I will deliver the Egyptians into the hand of a
hard master;
a fierce king will rule over them, says the Sovereign,
the Lord of hosts.

Isaiah 19:3, 4

Background information

Superstitions assume that there is a supernatural relationship of cause and effect between events even though there is no physical connection. It has therefore been associated with such things as witchcraft, magic and astrology. Religion itself has also been called a superstition. From the Enlightenment onwards any belief in miracles, the power of prayer, or prophecy, for example, was condemned as superstitious and much of Christian belief suffered from this judgement. Where religion itself was accepted and widely believed it was the religion of others that was deemed to be merely 'superstition'. In the Roman Empire outlawed cults were described in this way, as too was the Papacy by Martin Luther. In the King James version of the Bible the religion of the Athenians (Acts 17:22) is described by St Paul as 'superstition'. Christians often describe Voodoo as a superstition.

Superstitious behaviour seeks to avoid evil or promote 'good luck' and can even be contradictory in different settings, e.g. a black cat is generally thought to be 'bad luck' while sailors view it as 'good luck'. The world of sport and the theatre, perhaps because of the intensity of public display, are full of superstition. Cricketers will only put on their pads in a specific order, footballers wear the same shirt throughout a cup run, actors never wish each other good luck (they say 'break a leg') and if someone mentions Macbeth in the theatre the person has to go outside, spin round three times, spit, curse and knock to be let back in. The origin of such superstitions is not clear but some have obvious religious association, e.g. not having 13 people at a dinner table, or Friday as an unlucky day (sailors used to avoid setting sail on a Friday). Some superstitions reflect practical common sense, e.g. 'it is unlucky to walk under a ladder'.

Sermon ideas

'Good days', 'Bad days', 'Good luck', 'Bad luck' – we've experienced them all. Most people would like to avoid the bad experiences and encourage the good. It has always been that way and the search began long before the start of history for ways to influence events. Survival itself has sometimes been thought to depend on it. Stars have been consulted and so have old bones, wood has been touched for protection and certain numbers avoided to ward off evil. A piece of coal is offered for luck and heather sold to bring good fortune. Our enlightened world pronounces such things as 'mere superstition', yet thousands read the astrologers' predictions in the tabloids and even top politicians have been known to make decisions in the light of the position of the planets. Superstition, it seems, is alive and well.

But one person's superstition is another's deeply-held belief and one person's religious faith is another's superstition. From the point of view of the Jews with their firm and exclusive belief in Yahweh, the Lord of all, the beliefs of those who lived in neighbouring countries were simply superstition – relying, like the Egyptians, on worshipping pieces of wood or dependent on charms and sorcery, necromancy and spirits. The Jews were firmly commanded to have nothing to do with such nonsense (Deuteronomy18:9-14). There was but one God and following his word was the only way. All history and all the future were in his hands and faithfulness and obedience were what mattered if his people were to find good fortune and avoid evil. Not that that prevented them, of course, from dabbling in the ways of foreigners. Saul, at a time of crisis, consulted a witch and the 'spirit' of Samuel was conjured up (1 Samuel 28) and the mention of earrings among the ornaments worn by women is thought to refer to charms to ward off evil spirits (Isaiah 3:18-23).

The problem with superstitions is that on occasions they 'work'. A person wears a 'lucky' T shirt or bracelet and something good happens. The superstition is reinforced and the research of psychologists suggests that a reinforced belief is very hard to displace even though there may be frequent occasions when the 'lucky' T shirt produced no good result.

To the secular, enlightened mind many of the practices of Christians appear to be the product of superstition. For those who only accept 'scientific' explanations to account for behaviour and events, faith and its manifestations are irrational superstitions. Answers to prayer, miracles, empowerment by the Holy Spirit can all be scornfully dismissed. The fact that Christians can give evidence of prayer working does not overcome such scepticism. For the believer these things may be supra-rational but not therefore necessarily irrational. Faith in the end remains faith – not a simple matter of argument. The belief in God who is in all and through all and over all means that all our activity, all our search for good outcomes and the avoidance of evil begins and ends with him – not with rabbits' feet or avoiding cracks in the paving stone, not with the position of Venus nor crossing your fingers.

Story

During the 2012 Olympics an avid watcher of the television presentation assured astonished colleagues at a drinking session in a pub that he had been responsible for Andy Murray's defeat of Roger Federer to win the gold medal. When asked how this could be, he stated that it was only because he had moved from the left end of the sofa to the 'lucky' right end of the sofa during the match that Murray had won. He backed up this assertion with the comment that he had inadvertently been sitting at the left end of the sofa when Murray lost to Federer at Wimbledon just a month earlier.

Thought to take away

We do not destroy religion by destroying superstition. (Cicero)
The root of all superstition is that men observe when a thing hits, but not when it misses. (Francis Bacon)

Swearing

Robert Reiss

You shall not take the name of the Lord your God in vain; for the Lord will not hold him guiltless who takes his name in vain.

Exodus 20:7 (Revised Standard Version)

Background information

Most swear words find their origin either in blasphemous phrases, and so offend the third commandment, or have a sexual reference, which many find offensive on other grounds. For those reasons Christians have traditionally opposed their use. However, for some swear words the link with blasphemous phrases has been almost forgotten, 'bloody' for example is associated with the phrase 'by our Lady' (although that is disputed by some etymologists) but most people who use the word would not be aware of that association. A more relaxed approach to matters of sex has also changed the acceptability, at least for some, of the use of language with sexual connotations. In so far as the BBC acts as a barometer of social change, over the last fifty years there has been a move to allowing language now that would have been completely unacceptable in an earlier age.

Sermon ideas

While traditionally most Christians have opposed swearing, and many remain firmly opposed, there has been some relaxation in attitudes over recent years. There are at least four reasons for that relaxation.

First, the context makes a difference. Where swearing is very common, in some (but not all) workplaces for example, not to swear at all would be to stand out against the crowd. Some Christians would consider that always wholly right and proper, but others might be reluctant to appear unduly pious or even self-righteous, and would rather be identified as sharing a common culture. Each person must make their own decision about how to respond to their context, although when in a context where the use of such language would cause offence then it should certainly be avoided.

Secondly, in the appropriate place, to use a swear word can emphasise a point. It could well be argued that to use it in that way is simply a reflection of the lack of other more acceptable ways of emphasising something, which is why some have considered swearing simply a sign of an inadequate education. What is clear, though, is that the power of a word to emphasise something is lessened if it is used too frequently.

Thirdly, there are many situations in which a person might, quite reasonably, feel angry and to express that anger through the use of a swear word might in practice be part of an anger management technique. In such situations the use of words rather than other more violent reactions would certainly be more preferable, while bottling up anger can have other more destructive consequences. In such contexts swearing might well be the lesser of a number of evils.

Fourthly, some clinical psychological research at Keele University in 2011 indicated that when someone hurts themself, the use of swearing does actually lessen pain. It seems that there is a physiological effect generated by the use of swearing in such a situation.

Story

There have been a number of examples where famous people known for their respectability have been caught either on sound recordings or on film using language that to other people would be offensive. That certainly applied to President Nixon in the Watergate tapes and to Kevin Rudd, a former Prime Minister of Australia. For those to whom it causes offence it lessens the standing of that person, but for those who use such language themselves it can establish an empathetic link.

Thought to take away

Jesus asked us to love our neighbours as ourselves. We all have to make judgements on how our neighbours will react to our behaviour, and if something causes them offence it is unlikely to be received as an example of love. Caution about the use of bad language must be the most loving response.

Theft

Brian Fahy

A man in the crowd said to him, 'Master, tell my brother to give me a share of our inheritance.' 'My friend' he replied 'who appointed me your judge, or the arbitrator of your claims?' Then he said to them, 'Watch and be on your guard against avarice of any kind, for a man's life is not made secure by what he owns, even when he has more than he needs.

Luke 12:13-15 (Jerusalem Bible)

Background information

Wealth and poverty provide the background to this subject – the unequal distribution of wealth and resources in human life. It would be too easy to identify 'theft' with the simple category of burglary, pickpocketing or bank-robbing, serious as these offences are. The issue is far wider and deeper than that. When we speak of theft, we must also speak of human inequality, corruption in high places, of social injustice, and of our common tendency to greed and selfishness. These matters can make thieves of us all.

In the United Kingdom there was a 55 per cent fall in the rate of burglaries from the mid 1990s. Then, when the recession took hold, and with a rise in unemployment, personal theft crime rose by 25 per cent, and burglary by 4 per cent. These statistics bear out the Old Testament saying, that poverty may tempt us to steal (Proverbs 30:8, 9).

That temptation to steal is not confined to the poor, however. People with money are sorely tempted to hold on to it very tightly, and theft in this area takes the form of business fraud and tax avoidance. A TUC report claims that tax avoidance by individuals costs the Treasury £13 billion per year, and tax avoidance from business, £12 billion. This dwarfs the £1 billion loss caused by benefit fraud.

In an effort to raise our awareness, our consciousness of these issues, the Church has produced many documents on matters of social justice and common endeavour. 'Faith in the City' was produced by the Church of England in 1985, following urban riots in Britain, with a follow-up document, 'Faithful Cities' in 2006. Riots are often a shout for help, a violent protest against a life without hope or prospect. 'Faith in the City' gave a voice to people in such deprivation, and 'Faithful Cities' spoke about 'faithful capital' – the values and empowerments, the relationships and motivations that make community life possible.

Catholic Social Teaching, beginning with Rerum Novarum in 1891, has, in recent times produced Populorum Progressio (1967), Solicitudo Rei Socialis (1987) and Caritas in Veritate (2009). Central to this teaching is the idea of the 'common good'. Our life and our prosperity in this world must be inclusive of the needs of all people everywhere. We must have a particular care for the poor.

Sermon ideas

The Ten Commandments, given to Moses on Mount Sinai, are a valuable guide to living the good life. Yet, it is very easy to delude ourselves into thinking that some of those commands do not concern us very much. We are not thieves, we tell ourselves. A little dishonest in expenses, perhaps, on occasion, but not greatly at fault. Theft is such a serious word. But if we think of another word – selfishness, for instance, we can easily own up to that particular fault. And if we change that word and insert the word 'greed' – admittedly a much stronger word – we are still able to admit to that at times. And if we confess to greed, we confess to keeping to ourselves what could easily be given to, or shared with, another. There are many ways to be a thief!

The Church's social teaching begins with the claim that the goods of the world are originally meant for all. We are meant to share the goods of this world. Private property is valid and necessary, but it exists under a 'social mortgage'. This means that it has an intrinsically social function, that private property is not an absolute right, and that it exists in the context of the universal destination of the goods of the earth. Recent riots in Britain (2011), which saw great destruction of property, also produced an analysis that many thousands of people feel that they have no stake in society. They feel they do not belong. They have no resources, no opportunity to better themselves. This, in a society where some people earn huge amounts of money, living in a celebrity culture.

In recent years we have become accustomed to seeing some people become extremely rich, out of all proportion to the rest of society. We even come to accept this state of affairs, and some people live their dreams of wealth vicariously, following the life stories of the rich and famous. And yet we know that this gap between rich and poor is obscene. The dangers are that the wealthy look for ways to increase their wealth, and the poor are often driven to crime or violent protest. Our consumer society instils consumer attitudes in us all, encouraging us to consume goods that other people can only dream of.

The 'gap' between rich and poor, revealed by urban riots, is also well known in the wider world, where the rich North is divided from the poor South. Our human efforts to address this inequality are hampered by a 'lack of brotherhood between individuals and peoples' (Paul VI, Populorum Progressio). The great idea and goal for helping others, taught by the Church, is 'the Common Good', but this idea is greatly limited and hindered by the partisan attitudes of nations, looking to their own interests.

Instead of such narrowness of mind, the Christian Church urges people who are caught up in a world of consumerism and hedonism, to discover the joy of giving. The human race is a single family, and we owe it to one another to look out for each other and to share the goods we possess. Learn generosity of spirit. Learn solidarity of life. Remembering the parable of Jesus, let it not be said that we wined and dined while others starved at our gate (Luke 16:19-31).

Story

A man stood in an airport terminal, with his fellow cruise ship travellers, waiting for his luggage to be delivered for transfer to his flight. When the luggage arrived, there was a sudden commotion as people moved together to retrieve their suitcases. Somebody bumped into the man, and immediately he knew he had been robbed. His wallet had been stolen from his trouser pocket. Quickly he recognised the stranger he had seen earlier, walking away from the crowd, and he knew he was the culprit. He grabbed him tightly and insisted on his wallet being returned. He heard a sound. It was his wallet falling to the ground from underneath the stranger's overcoat. He picked up his wallet and let the pickpocket go.

Later he reflected on how angry he felt about this incident. 'Am I too possessive?' he asked himself. 'Why do I feel so very angry about this?' After much thought he concluded, 'No, I am not overly possessive. I am angry because this man does not respect me, or anything that belongs to me, be it money, or the photograph of my son that I keep in my wallet.' Property is not only things, possessions. Property means everything that is proper to me – my place in this world, my right to share in this world, my dignity as a person. It is about honour and respect.

Thought to take away

The Book of Proverbs contains a prayer asking that we be neither rich nor poor (Proverbs 30:8, 9). Wealth would make us forgetful of God. Poverty could tempt us to theft. Let us be content with shelter, food and clothing, and learn to live in solidarity and generosity with all.

Tokenism

Edgar Ruddock

'Unless I see the mark of the nails in his hands, and put my finger in the mark of the nails and my hand in his side, I will not believe.'

John 20:25

Background information

Consider these facts:

- There is a glass ceiling for women in business, or for black officers in the police force.
- Appointments are still sometimes made to give as good an impression as possible of a Board regarding equal opportunities, rather than being made on a candidate's merit or potential.
- A high percentage of Britons still put 'Church of England' on official forms, though few if any will regularly attend church.
- We put coppers in the charity box to salve our conscience, not because we believe in fundamental change.

There is a big gap between giving something the nod and being fully committed to it!

Sermon ideas

When Thomas was confronted by the other disciples with the news that Jesus was alive, was he really wrestling with deep doubt? Or was he in fact wanting to keep the reality of what was happening at arm's length, in order to allow himself to come to terms with what had happened, shrug and move on? To his shock and dismay then, a week later, Jesus appears again and invites Thomas to do the very thing he was secretly wanting to avoid. To face facts.

Then, as he puts his hands gingerly close to those of Jesus, and engages the nail prints, and puts his hand into Jesus' side, suddenly he comes face to face with the reality of all the pain and suffering that Jesus has gathered into his own sacrificial death. And for Thomas, this is the moment of truth! His famous words 'My Lord and my God!' are not just about overcoming doubt: they are a much more profound realisation that you cannot bring about transformation and change – either cosmically or locally – without there being a real price to pay. And as he begins to understand, he indicates his willingness to be part of the change he wants to see in the world.

For so many people, leaders especially, change is about dressing things up in the best light, often as much to protect reputations and power, as to make a real difference. But now Thomas puts his hand right into the places of pain, finds Jesus to be really there, and commits himself to be part of the process of transformation. Not 'You are truly God!' but '*my* Lord and *my* God!'

Story

Go back a few days in the story of the Passion. In John's account (John 13:5-9) Jesus has gathered with his disciples for their shared meal. He gets up from the table, lays aside his garments, and washes his disciples' feet. Peter of course, ever impetuous, says 'No chance! You're not going to wash my feet!' No doubt he says it in respect for Jesus as the leader and teacher of the group. But Jesus' response is to the point: 'Unless I wash your feet you can have no part of me.' In other words, 'Peter, you can't stand on the edge of this, and just be a passenger . . . You're in it with us all, or you are not.' And Peter's response is, 'Not just my feet then, but my hands and my head also!' In other words he suddenly tumbles to the realisation that being with, and following Jesus is no armchair activity. It is about total commitment, and a revolutionary lifestyle. And history showed how true that was for him.

Thought to take away

Following Jesus in the twenty-first century calls for a radical rethink about how we live, and how we fit into our society. There is so much humbug uttered by people who claim the moral and political high ground. Sometimes we are tempted to say, 'Well then, it's best to keep my head down, avoid the accusation of being a hypocrite, and mind my own business.' If Thomas, Peter, and countless courageous saints down the centuries had done that (including in recent decades and generations) then we would have no gospel to proclaim, and the world would be a poorer place by far.

Travellers and gypsies

Edgar Ruddock

Then you shall declare before the Lord your God: 'My father was a wandering Aramean.'

Deuteronomy 26:5 (New International Version)

Background information

There are somewhere between 180,000 and 300,000 travellers in the UK today (some of whom will also be householders).

There are distinctive communities whose roots have been in Ireland, Scotland, Eastern Europe and elsewhere. Some of their histories go back many centuries: remnants of communities displaced by migration or war; the Irish Parvee peoples, often known as gypsies or tinkers (sellers of pots and pans); gypsies whose forebears travelled from central Europe or even from Egypt (hence the name); the Romany peoples whose roots can be traced through Europe to the Indian sub-continent. And of course, today there is also a sizeable travelling community whose roots are in the New Age Movement.[54]

Sermon ideas

If we go far enough back in history, we will discover that most of our ancestors were at some point of nomadic stock. Early man was a hunter gatherer, a wanderer, before the discovery of grain farming led to the arrival of more settled communities.

For the Jews, the experience of the Exodus, and the years of wandering in the wilderness, became their great paradigm of faith: they were a travelling people, and God was their travelling Companion. While they longed to settle, they always held alive the memory of their journeying history.

Later the Gospel writers over and over again described the details of Jesus' journeys through Galilee and towards Jerusalem. 'While they were on the way . . .' was a common introductory phrase to the next story, parable or encounter. This is no coincidence.

People of faith will therefore have a special place in their hearts for those whose lives are less rooted, and more mobile, than many others. There is much to learn in being free of baggage, being more flexible in facing life's challenges and disappointments. As Jesus told his disciples as he sent them out in pairs, 'Take no second coat for your backs . . .' (Mark 6:8; Luke 9:3).

This is not to say of course, that travellers have it all right and the rest of us have no idea! There is great value in being settled, seeing things through, engaging with local communities, being there for the long haul to make a difference etc.

Some key questions emerge then, for thinking Christians:

- Are we so dependent on our possessions, homes and security, that we are never free to respond to God's call, or God's divine will for our lives?
- What is at the root of our anxiety over travellers and gypsies?
- Do we fear difference, object to 'irresponsibility', or simply dislike any threat to the order of our comfortable world?
- How can we make our churches places of welcome for those who travel?
- Can we help our schools support those families whose children have fewer opportunities for formal education because of their circumstances?
- Can we listen more sensitively to those who feel that they are excluded from normal society more by society's prejudice, than by their own choices?
- How does a view of Jesus as the archetypal traveller inform our understanding of the Good News of the gospel?

Story

What was going on in the 2012 stand-off at Dale Farm, where bailiffs and local travellers came head to head in ugly scenes? Local people objected to the informal expansion of a legally agreed site for travellers. The case came to court and the travellers were ordered to comply with the regulations. As they resisted, bailiffs and police were mobilised, and a wider community gathered to support the travellers. There was real danger of prolonged conflict. This raises the question of how we as Christians learn to live with difference. In the Old Testament, Cain, the settled farmer found one solution to the threat of damage to his crops by killing his nomadic brother Abel. How does the life and ministry of Jesus call for a very different solution? What shape might it take in your community?

Thought to take away

Pilgrims have always encountered God along the way, as they face challenges, dangers, and hardships – what does it mean to let go of our securities and learn to be a follower, a pilgrim? And in so following, might we just find others?

54. See this link: http://www.bemis.org.uk/resources/gt/scotland/Beth%20Cadger%20-%20gypsytraveller%20numbers%20in%20the%20UK%20%20a%20general%20overview.pdf

Usury

Rupert Bristow

One who augments wealth by exorbitant interest gathers it for another who is kind to the poor.

Proverbs 28:8

Background information

Many years ago Private Eye used to produce scurrilous Christmas records to accompany the magazine. One of these featured a rather portentous voice, obviously designed to give the impression of being a priest, saying something along the lines of: 'At this festive season, let us not forget the real meaning of Christmas, the *commercial* meaning. As it written '. . . and there shall come a great profit throughout the land . . .' Point made, cue laughter, albeit rather uncomfortable laughter. It is still a moot point whether at Christmas people see the role of 'prophet' or 'profit' as more important!

But the banking and financial crisis has changed our perceptions of the security of money held for us, the assured interest on our savings, even the wisdom of the banks who hold our money that they will invest it efficiently, ethically – or either! And, just as people hark back to a Health Service 'golden age' largely in the hands of a 'ward sister' who actually cared about the patient and would take responsibility for the quality of care provided, so the judgement and wisdom of the person known as 'the bank manager' have attained almost mythic proportions.

Bad lending to the poor – known as sub-prime lending – has spread contagion in the financial system, compounded by mis-sold insurances, reckless rogue traders, obscene bonuses to investment bank staff and senior executives – and the spectre of the collapse of the whole financial system. The time seems right to rehabilitate the prophetic over the pursuit of profit.

Sermon ideas

As is often the case, the Book of Proverbs pithily and plainly states the case against excessive interest rates and warns that it will end in the money wrongly earned being returned to the poor. Would that were the case, though it could be argued that taxation, fines, state take-over or share-holder rebellion could result in money earned by dubious and reckless means, by those who already have enough money, losing their gains. These could then be recycled to those less well off through government subsidies, social support or some other form of redistribution. But equally, the interest – and possibly the sum itself – might also be lost entirely.

While the Bible sets out certain rules, such as not charging interest to the poor (Exodus 22:25) or to friends and family (Deuteronomy 23:20), and not charging excessive rates (Proverbs 28:8), there was an understanding from the Middle Ages in England, and explicitly in a 1554 Act under Henry VIII, that it is permissable to charge interest on lent money. And certainly because the exaction of a reasonable interest for a loan has been tolerated by the Christian Church, the term 'usury' has tended to be restricted to charging excessive rates. So, while we are left with images of Jesus overturning the tables of the money-changers (John 2:15), we are also confronted with the clear message of the Parable of the Talents (Matthew 25:14-30), that growing money by investing it is good practice. Of course the parable had a wider meaning about making sure we make full use of the gifts God has given us, yet it also makes clear that the wise and brave use of both talents and money is expected of us by God.

As Christians, as either a borrower or a lender (ignoring Polonius' advice in Hamlet that we should be neither), we need to demonstrate responsibility rather than greed, good money management rather than profligacy. We can't all become prodigal sons and hope to rely on the grace of God and the forgiveness of less reckless friends and family!

There is a school of thought that suggests that if we get our behaviour right, perhaps by regulation and the threat of penalties, then the problem will go away. Experience, however, suggests that the more all-encompassing regulation gets, the more people will use their ingenuity to find ways of avoiding it. Just as Jesus castigated the scribes and Pharisees about the minutiae of the Law for being more concerned with issues of ritual and practice rather than the bigger picture of the kingdom of God, so it seems that we all have a responsibility to get our underpinning values and principles right, if we are to turn things round, in ourselves as in society as a whole.

And that's where the transforming love of Jesus, his death for us all on the cross, and his resurrection from the dead are, quite simply, the basis on which we need to show in thought and word and deed how we honour his name and abide by his teaching.

Story

One way we can put this into practice is to give every member of the congregation up for the challenge £10 or £20 or £50 (depending on the confidence of your PCC treasurer!) and ask that in six months or a year it is turned into £100 or £200 or £500! But there is a warning note to this: if too many interesting and attractive things are made available for sale at the back of church towards this effort, there will be those who invoke the money-changers analogy to ban such sales! Where would you stand on this?

Thought to take away

Even if we accept the lessons of the Bible about avoiding usury and are careful in our personal financial dealings, should we not be sure that our neighbour, in the widest sense in this global age, is not disadvantaged by the use of the finances that we have borrowed or lent – or more particularly perhaps, by the interest earned by the financial intermediaries, i.e. the banks and the corporations? Do we hold them to account in the way that Jesus held the scribes, the Pharisees and the money-changers to account; and do we help and care for the poor person, the prisoner, the Samaritan, the tax-collector, the sinner, the prodigal son? As Christians we should surely do both.

Vivisection

Deborah Jones

And I heard every creature in heaven and on earth and under the earth and in the sea, and all therein, saying, 'To him who sits upon the throne and to the Lamb be blessing and honour and glory and might for ever and ever!'

Revelation 5:13 (Revised Standard Version)

Background information

Since the Enlightenment, and under the influence of Descartes' mistaken view that animals cannot feel pain, vivisection, living animals used in laboratory experiments, has been practised universally. Billions of animals, mainly rodents but also species such as dogs, cats, monkeys and many others, anaesthetised and not, are used for surgical procedures or for product testing, especially for medical drugs, but also for almost everything people handle. It is a generally-held legal requirement that tests be done on animals before new products can be brought to market. The animals suffer pain, acute stress, and premature death. Many scientists oppose the practice as animals are very poor indicators of human reactions and as alternative methods of testing are far more reliable, as well as more humane.

Sermon ideas

What is the Christian response to the use of animals in that way? The Bible gives little specific guidance as vivisection did not exist before the period of the Enlightenment, when the absurd notion developed that animals could feel no pain. This view widely influenced scientific practice and, while nobody nowadays accepts that idea, the custom of using animals still persists. Whether or not their pain *matters* is the question nowadays, and over this, Christians are divided.

What the Bible does give are several examples of God making covenants with his animal creation (Genesis 9:9; Hosea 2:18; Isaiah 54:9, 10). The book of Revelation, too, gives us a picture of animals of all kinds worshipping around the throne of God (Revelation 5:13). These passages remind us that God created animals first of all for God's direct relationship with them. They are God's, not ours.

There is a triangular relationship of love and compassion – between God and us, God and animals, and us and animals. When any one of these is distorted and deformed, the symmetry is broken. In Isaiah 11:5-9, we get a glimpse of the 'peaceable kingdom', the ideal restoration of Eden, when humans, animals and God will all cohabit peacefully and none harm the other. For to harm those who cannot defend themselves, is, in the words of John Henry Newman, 'satanic', and no Christian could endorse any such cruelty. The writer C. S. Lewis considered that 'The victory of vivisection marks a great advance in the triumph of ruthless, non-moral utilitarianism over the old world of ethical law.' Animals cannot give or withhold their consent, so that all harmful acts are imposed on them, as a bully might terrorise a smaller child.

While some understand animals as being God's own creatures, not belonging to us, and so not ours to abuse, others take the view that, so long as benefits to humans are directly attributable to this use, there is justification, even though there is a Christian axiom that 'one may not do evil so that good may result from it'. Here modern science indicates that, in fact, the use of animals is actually counterproductive in many fields, as one leading laboratory puts the results between animal tests and human results as failing a staggering 75 to 95 per cent of the time. Drugs tests are particularly unreliable compared with cell culture toxicology methods, and in other cases technological modelling is far more effective.

Story

In Shakespeare's play, Cymbeline, the wicked queen asks the physician, Cornelius, for some drugs to kill her husband slowly. She suggests that she should try them out 'on such creatures as/we count not worth the hanging – but none human'. Cornelius is shocked: 'Your Highness/shall from this practice but make hard your heart;/besides, the seeing these effects will be/both noisome [disgusting, harmful] and infectious' (I:5:19ff).

Thought to take away

One eminent professor of surgery at Harvard University, declared in the last century that, 'There will come a time when the world will look back to modern vivisection in the name of science as they now do to burning at the stake in the name of religion.'

Wealth

Paul Nicholson

Then all the elders of Israel gathered together and came to Samuel at Ramah, and said to him, 'You are old and your sons do not follow in your ways; appoint for us, then, a king to govern us, like other nations.' . . . So Samuel reported all the words of the Lord to the people who were asking him for a king. He said, 'These will be the ways of the king who will reign over you: he will take your sons and appoint them to his chariots and to be his horsemen, and to run before his chariots; and he will appoint for himself commanders of thousands and commanders of fifties, and some to plough his ground and to reap his harvest, and to make his implements of war and the equipment of his chariots. He will take your daughters to be perfumers and cooks and bakers. He will take the best of your fields and vineyards and olive orchards and give them to his courtiers. He will take one-tenth of your grain and of your vineyards and give it to his officers and his courtiers. He will take your male and female slaves, and the best of your cattle and donkeys, and put them to his work. He will take one-tenth of your flocks, and you shall be his slaves. And in that day you will cry out because of your king, whom you have chosen for yourselves; but the Lord will not answer you in that day.' But the people refused to listen to the voice of Samuel; they said, 'No! But we are determined to have a king over us, so that we also may be like other nations.'

1 Samuel 8: 4, 5, 10-20

Background information

A 2006 United Nations report[55], the largest ever undertaken into global distribution of wealth, concluded that the richest 1 per cent of the world's people own 40 per cent of the planet's wealth, and the richest 10 per cent own 85 per cent of it. By contrast, the bottom half of the world's population had to make do with only 1 per cent of global wealth. Wealth in this sense means more than simply earned or unearned income. It represents 'the value of physical and financial assets less liabilities', i.e. capital. By this measure, the United States is the richest country, with mean per capita wealth estimated at $144,000 in 2000; at the other end of the spectrum, the corresponding figure for India was $6,500. The United Kingdom came near to the top of the list, with capital per head of $129,000. The report estimated that the total wealth of the world at the millennium was $125 trillion.

Sermon ideas

It would be easy to preach a sermon attacking the richest 1 per cent in the figures above, backed up by such well-known scripture texts as, 'It is easier for a camel to go through the eye of a needle than for someone who is rich to enter the kingdom of God' (Luke 18:25), or 'The love of money is a root of all kinds of evil' (1 Timothy 6:10). In warning the people of Israel against their wish for a king, much of God's concern centres on the wealth that he will amass, and indeed, the third in the line of these monarchs who were eventually appointed, Solomon, is remembered for his fabulous wealth as well as for his fabled wisdom.

Yet wealth, and the creation of wealth, is not attacked in this passage from 1 Samuel. It is good that there are people tending to grain-fields, olive orchards and vineyards, breeding cattle and donkeys, cooking, baking, and crafting perfume. Society would be poorer without them and, indeed, one of the fears raised is that all will be impoverished if too many of these productive citizens are diverted into military occupations. By sharing in God's work of creation – part of what it means to be fashioned 'in the image and likeness of God' – human beings are called to be productive, and in this way to produce wealth.

Two things stand at the heart of the Bible's concern about wealth. The first is its concentration into the hands of a few, thereby denying the majority what they need to live decent lives. This is seen as akin to robbery; the rich have taken from the poor what is rightfully theirs. In doing so, at the extreme, they reduce the poor to a state little better than slavery. This is something that God, who takes the side of the poor in this kind of situation, will not tolerate. It is what Samuel fears in counselling against kingship, and it is graphically illustrated on a global level in the 2006 United Nations report.

The other concern that the Bible has when considering wealth is its tendency to lead people to focus on it, and its acquisition, to the exclusion of God. The love of money becomes the root of all evil when it distracts people from all that is involved in loving God in the practices of their everyday lives. In asking for a king the people are seen as rejecting God, who should be enthroned at the centre of the nation.

So wealth is good, and creating wealth can be a valid way of serving God. But wealth remains a powerful force, capable of leading people to focus on it to the exclusion of all else, and to sacrifice the poor in the process. Christians are unwise to simply attack wealth or the wealthy; but caution in approaching it, and an attitude that questions how the wealthy acquired and use their wealth, is clearly to be encouraged.

Story

There is a saying, variously attributed, but seemingly coming from a Native American source, that succinctly sums up the limitations of the view of wealth most common in much of the developed world:

> When the last tree is cut,
> the last fish is caught,
> and the last river is polluted;
> when to breathe the air is sickening,
> you will realise, too late,
> that wealth is not in bank accounts
> and that you can't eat money.

Thought to take away

Most readers of this book will be well up the scale in the listings of global wealth. Yet wealth represents power, and with power comes responsibility. Fruitless guilt over this situation is an easy, yet unproductive, response. What responsibility, particularly to those who are poorer than myself, might my wealth be pointing me towards?

---

55. James B. Davies et al, *The World Distribution of Household Wealth*. World Institute for Development Economics Research of the United Nations, 2006. Accessed at www.lisproject.org/lws/introduction/finalconf/06.1%20Davies-Sandstrom-Shorrocks-Wolff.pdf, 2 July 2012.

World hunger

Paul Nicholson

Elijah set out and went to Zarephath. When he came to the gate of the town, a widow was there gathering sticks; he called to her and said, 'Bring me a little water in a vessel, so that I may drink.' As she was going to bring it, he called to her and said, 'Bring me a morsel of bread in your hand.' But she said, 'As the Lord your God lives, I have nothing baked, only a handful of meal in a jar, and a little oil in a jug; I am now gathering a couple of sticks, so that I may go home and prepare it for myself and my son, that we may eat it, and die.' Elijah said to her, 'Do not be afraid; go and do as you have said; but first make me a little cake of it and bring it to me, and afterwards make something for yourself and your son. For thus says the Lord the God of Israel: The jar of meal will not be emptied and the jug of oil will not fail until the day that the Lord sends rain on the earth.'

1 Kings 17:10-14

Background information

According to the website of the World Food Programme of the United Nations, globally 925 million people (13.2 per cent of the world's population) are seriously undernourished. Currently 10.9 million children under 5 die in developing countries each year, and malnutrition and hunger-related diseases cause 60 per cent of these deaths. The first of the Millennium Development Goals, agreed by all the signatories to the United Nations charter, included the resolve to halve the proportion of the world's population suffering from extreme hunger between 1990 and 2015. Although progress has been made, much more needs to be done if this goal is to be reached.

Sermon ideas

For those of us living in more affluent parts of the world, it is easy to respond to world hunger in two ways. The first is to feel overwhelmed by the scale of the problem. It seems too big, and too complex, for me as an individual, or even my local community, to do anything effective about. The temptation then is to turn my attention elsewhere and do nothing, perhaps meanwhile making a charitable donation to one of the aid agencies as a way of salving my conscience. The second response, which may follow the first, is to feel guilty. 'Feeding the hungry' is, after all, an injunction found repeatedly in the Bible, and it is difficult to argue that it doesn't apply to me.

The story of Elijah's response to the widow of Zarephath can illustrate one way of moving beyond this impasse. As Jesus later points out (see Luke 4:25, 26), this widow was not alone at the time in suffering the effects of drought and famine. Yet the prophet does not attempt to feed all the hungry, or establish a large-scale programme to care for them. He does what he can, with God's help, for one family whom he encounters. Not everyone in Israel at the time will have been able to channel God's miraculous power in the way that Elijah did. But if everyone had done whatever they could, with God's help, we may assume that the situation would have been vastly improved. It is surely better to start with some small-scale concrete action than to agonise fruitlessly about the wider situation.

Beyond that, Christians (and indeed members of other faiths) have a good track record of establishing and maintaining agencies which will make a wider difference, through lobbying and campaigning, the gathering and distribution of resources, and education. Organisations such as Oxfam and CAFOD rely on the support of church members in a variety of ways – not simply through giving money – to continue their work. Discovering how, in my own situation, I can best support them is likely to be one way of 'feeding the hungry'. Simply informing myself more fully, with the help of the excellent resources that many of these agencies produce, can be a large first step in addressing these issues.

Story

Early in the Second World War, Greece was occupied by Nazi forces. In response the Allies created a naval blockade around the country to prevent further German expansion. So effective was this, that it resulted in starvation among Greek civilians, and particularly women and children. In 1942 a Famine Relief Committee, based in the university church of St Mary the Virgin in Oxford, was established to ship emergency supplies through the blockade to alleviate the situation. Its identification code in the telegraphic system of the time was 'Oxfam', and after the war it expanded its operations to help the situation of war-ravaged Europe. Since 1994 Oxfam International has been a global aid agency creating a network from 16 national organisations.

Thought to take away

Hunger need not always be a bad thing. At its most basic level, it serves to alert us to those times when we need nourishment. Furthermore, in Matthew's version of the Beatitudes, Jesus declares, 'Blessed are those who hunger and thirst for righteousness, for they will be filled' (Matthew 5:6). What God-given hungers do you find within yourself, spurring you on in your journey towards the kingdom of God?

Index of Bible texts

Mark 14:3-9	Deprivation
Luke 6:36	Euthanasia
Luke 6:41, 42	Anti-Semitism
Luke 12:13-15	Theft
Luke 15:17-24	Responsibility
Luke 15:18, 19	Guilt
Luke 18:15-17	Embryology
Luke 23:44-46a	Rape
John 1:43-46	Discrimination
John 4:27	Prejudice
John 5:2-9	Healing
John 8:7-11	Aids/HIV
John 8:31, 32	Hypocrisy
John 14:6	Scandal
John 15:12	Organ transplant
John 20:19	Reconciliation
John 20:25	Tokenism
Acts 10:15	Multi-culturalism
Acts 16:16-19	Fortune-telling
Romans 3:22b-25a	Prison
Romans 12:1, 2	Sterilisation
Romans 15:1-3	Censorship
1 Corinthians 1:24	Power
1 Corinthians 6:13b-20	Promiscuity
1 Corinthians 9:24, 25	Discipline
1 Corinthians 9:24-27	Abstinence
1 Corinthians 15:58	Responsible behaviour
Ephesians 4:5, 6	Adoption
Ephesians 4:17-24	Lust
Philippians 2:3, 4	Ambition
1 Timothy 6:10	Money
1 Timothy 6:16, 17	Risk
Hebrews 4:12, 13	Lying
James 3:8-10	Gossip
1 Peter 4:12, 13	Pain
1 John 3:17, 18	Hunger
1 John 4:16-18	Islamophobia
Revelation 5:13	Vivisection
Revelation 7:13-17	Persecution